Robert Dessaix is a writer, translator, broadcaster and essayist. From 1985 to 1995, after teaching Russian language and literature for many years at the Australian National University and the University of New South Wales, he presented the weekly *Books and Writing* program on ABC Radio National. In more recent years he has also presented radio series on Australian public intellectuals and great travellers in history, as well as regular programs on language. His best-known books, all translated into several European languages, are his autobiography *A Mother's Disgrace*, the novels *Night Letters* and *Corfu*, a collection of essays and short stories *(and so forth)* and the travel memoirs *Twilight of Love* and *Arabesques*. A full-time writer since 1995, Robert Dessaix lives in Hobart, Tasmania.

Also by Robert Dessaix

Fiction
Night Letters: a Journey through Switzerland and Italy
Corfu

Non-fiction
A Mother's Disgrace
Secrets with Drusilla Modjeska and Amanda Lohrey
(and so forth)
Twilight of Love: Travels with Turgenev
Arabesques: a Tale of Double Lives
On Humbug

Edited
Picador New Writing
Australian Gay and Lesbian Writing: an Anthology
Speaking Their Minds: Intellectuals and the Public Culture in Australia
The Best Australian Essays 2004
The Best Australian Essays 2005

ROBERT DESSAIX

As I was saying

A COLLECTION OF MUSINGS

VINTAGE BOOKS
Australia

A Vintage book
Published by Random House Australia Pty Ltd
Level 3, 100 Pacific Highway, North Sydney NSW 2060
www.randomhouse.com.au

First published by Vintage in 2012

Copyright © Robert Dessaix 2012

The author and publisher are grateful to the following for permission to reproduce copyright material: Sarah Day and Brandl & Schlesinger for 'Cat Bird' from *Grass Notes*; Alfred A. Knopf and Anvil Press Poetry for 'Here in Katmandu' by Donald Justice; Faber & Faber Ltd for the lines from 'Annus mirabilis' by Philip Larkin; The Society of Authors (UK) for Edward Forster's letter to Mohammed el Adl.

The moral right of the author has been asserted.

All rights reserved. No part of this book may be reproduced or transmitted by any person or entity, including internet search engines or retailers, in any form or by any means, electronic or mechanical, including photocopying (except under the statutory exceptions provisions of the Australian *Copyright Act 1968*), recording, scanning or by any information storage and retrieval system without the prior written permission of Random House Australia.

Addresses for companies within the Random House Group can be found at
www.randomhouse.com.au/offices

National Library of Australia
Cataloguing-in-Publication Entry

Dessaix, Robert, 1944–

As I was saying / Robert Dessaix

ISBN 978 1 74275 307 2 (pbk)

A828.3

Cover images: dogs sitting on elegant chairs © Eric Raotosh Photography / Getty Images / Photolibrary; *Decoration of the Camera degli Sposi* by Mantegna Andrea © Photoservice Electa / Getty Images / Photolibrary
Cover design by Gayna Murphy
Typeset in 11.5/16 Adobe Garamond by Midland Typesetters, Australia
Printed and bound by Griffin Press, South Australia, an accredited ISO AS/NZS 14001:2004 Environmental Management System printer

The paper this book is printed on is certified against the Forest Stewardship Council® Standards. Griffin Press holds FSC chain of custody certification SGS-COC-005088. FSC promotes environmentally responsible, socially beneficial and economically viable management of the world's forests.

I'm sitting in my tower, cogitating. Not meditating – I never meditate, I don't have the knack – but rambling in my mind, alert to unexpected provocations. The mountain to the west, I see, is misting over.

It's not a real tower. How could it be? There aren't any real towers in the town I live in, just a few belvederes, some with a widow's walk. Merely glancing up at a widow's walk as you pass by, even on the brightest morning, can make you feel mournful. This was once a whaling town, where the whalers' wives – or so the story goes – paced round and round on these curious little balconies, watching, sometimes in vain, for their husbands' ships to come sailing up the estuary. This is humbug. No whaler's wife was ever sighted pacing one of these miniature balconies. Widow's walks are just architectural frippery. All the same, they strike an appealingly melancholy note in the lusher, seaside suburbs of towns from Portland, Maine to Hobart in Tasmania.

Vita Sackville-West, on the other hand, did have a real tower to think and write poetry in – an Elizabethan one, no less, at Sissinghurst in Kent. Her writing room is still there, apparently (I've yet to see it), with everything just as she left it: oak desk, old French tapestry, photograph of Virginia Woolf, Moroccan dagger, matches, letters, books, all still infused with the smell of mown grass that wafts up the staircase in spring and summer. In his book *Sissinghurst*, her grandson, Adam Nicolson, who still lives at Sissinghurst, describes this room as a vision of 'gradual withdrawal', a kind of 'bass line of music in which the high notes were the growing and flowering of the garden', the famous white garden surrounding the tower. That is vital in any tower refuge, real or imaginary: the bassoon-like melancholy of the room itself (tower rooms being always slightly gloomy, even the ones built inside your head) must be offset by livelier notes from outside – in Montaigne's case, for instance, over in France, everything from clanking wine presses to wandering troupes of acrobats; in my case today, more prosaically, workmen building an attic across the road and the chatter of passers-by.

The door at the bottom of the wooden stairway was locked while Vita worked, as was the door to the room itself. When she was writing, she did not 'come down'. She did invite friends up into it, it's true, but the herd was kept at bay, as was her husband, who only visited her in it four times.

That is a proper tower.

Somewhere there amongst Vita's books – the gardening books, the history books, the memoirs, the poetry, the musings on sex and so on – there is sure to be a volume of W. B. Yeats (possibly *The Tower*). How could there not be? After all, one of her lovers,

Dorothy Wellesley, Duchess of Wellington and decidedly minor poet, became Yeats's fast friend. Now, Yeats, too, had a proper tower, a square one, Thor Ballylee, beside the Cloon River in County Galway. It was also sixteenth-century, and I haven't seen it, either. There at the top of a narrow, winding stair is the 'chamber arched with stone' where, in summer, Yeats spun his magic. No matter how he began, he said, 'it becomes love poetry before I am finished with it'. Nothing but a heron or stray beggar ever disturbed his peace there.

In the actual sixteenth century, near Bordeaux, Michel de Montaigne famously thought and wrote on the top floor of a much older white stone tower with a pointed roof. He also died in it, but not on the top floor. In his library under the attic, surrounded by books, family heirlooms and a whole cabinet of curiosities (including swords, bracelets, even beds) from South America, he spent twenty years working on the first essays ever penned in Europe whose real subject was the writer's fluctuating self. Here he 'paid court' to himself, as he put it. He liked to walk about as well, as I do, in order to unjumble his mind. 'My thoughts fall asleep if I make them sit down,' he wrote. 'My mind will not budge unless my legs move it.' But you have to sit down in your tower to give your thoughts shape. He touched on almost everything in his *Essays*, from the armour of the Parthians to thumbs, but his core subject was his own becoming. Montaigne, a staunch Christian for all his fluctuating, would no doubt have thought of it as his undulating soul, a notion I'm quite partial to, holding as I do to the wave theory of the self as opposed to the particle theory favoured by most theologians. His tower, still standing, was his refuge, his bastion, in times of almost inconceivable savagery in France – wars, massacres, burnings, hangings, famine and banditry – especially in and around nearby Bordeaux.

In quieter times, Rilke had an odd little tower of sorts (it doesn't quite *tower*) for writing elegies and sonnets in at his Château de Muzot in Switzerland. And, not far away, in Bollingen, Carl Jung built his own tower, also real (but only just), beside Lake Zurich, imagining it represented the structure of the human consciousness. The effect is Disneyesque. There may be a lesson in that.

You don't have to be Carl Jung, though, to grasp that a tower is rarely just a tower. In the case of my tower, it's not even a tower. My tower is entirely fanciful. All the same, some have said that you can see it from quite a long way away.

I feel a bond with these turriphiliacs – Montaigne, Rilke, Vita Sackville-West and all the others, going right the way back to St Simeon the Stylite, who sat alone on top of a series of pillars on a hill outside Aleppo for forty years in the fifth century, rejecting the world and becoming so famous that even Buñuel made a film about him. I feel less of a bond with St Simeon, I admit, than with Vita Sackville-West, say, who was a gardener and a lesbian – all I could think, to be honest, when I stood recently staring at the stump of one of his pillars in the ruins of his basilica in the middle of nowhere was that he must have been barking mad – but still, I do feel a link, even if my tower is just in my head. There's a faint echo of all those real towers in my hilltop retreat – the weavings and carpets and pots from far-off places, a celadon bowl, the wooden cleaver from the Sepik, whole walls of books – but when I call my room a 'tower' I'm just daydreaming. I know that.

At the heart of it is not so much disdain for the crowd, as an aversion to it. There's a difference. At root we do not trust mass society in our times. We think it is degenerate and always on the verge of violence, as discos are, as well as shopping malls and a certain kind of pub on a Friday night. (Whether we're right about this or not, whether contemporary art, music, architecture, literature, conversation and mores in general are really in a state of decay or just a muddle as they always were, is neither here nor there. It's what we *feel*.) It's not that we feel contempt for Western society as a whole, we are not the kind to go off in disgust to try living off nature in an abandoned bus in the Alaskan wilderness, like Chris McCandless, who died four months later of starvation, quite unnecessarily, even stupidly, and had a film made about him by Sean Penn. We just want to withdraw from time to time, especially in the morning, from the crowd and its noisy culture. We seek to rise above it all. So, in one form or another, we build towers. The solitude you experience in a tower is not the hermit's, though: it is shot through with an exhilarating sense of control. You are alone in it, but still central, with views across your entire estate. You are not *cooped up*.

You might come down from your eyrie in the afternoon – Montaigne, Vita and Yeats had winding staircases to climb down, St Simeon had a ladder visitors climbed up after lunch (I've seen a carving of it) – to mingle with the world, delight the senses, fall in love, go shopping and amble about. In fact, seclusion past noon can be a dicey business. Even monks and hermits knew that. Around twelve, as the Scythian monk John Cassian recognised fifteen hundred years ago, torpor was apt to strike. But in the morning you can still befriend yourself in delicious seclusion in your sanctuary, ordering your thoughts and finding the right words for things. In the morning silence and solitude can seem mysteriously full. Children (although not dogs) must clearly be kept at bay, indeed most of my turriphiliacs either had no children or ignored the ones they had. The time spent in your tower is for belonging to yourself alone.

These days, however, unless you're an aristocrat or an anchorite, which few of us are, it's extraordinarily difficult to hide away undisturbed in your tower, even for a morning. Towers themselves have gone out of fashion, for that matter: from once being the fortified heart of the estate, illumined at night by hundreds of candles like soaring sources of radiance in the boundless dark, they turned bit by bit into empty follies perched on rises in the park. Even if you do have a tower at your disposal, or a mind with an upper chamber, the clatter and clang of the world below have a way of barging their way up the winding staircase and into your sanctuary these days, more or less at will. And you half want them to, especially towards lunchtime.

Yet the sheen of thought needs to stay unruffled (doesn't it?). Otherwise we – *we* – risk failing to take shape, like reflections on a pond, *as us*, even for a moment. And unless you have a tower to retreat into, a moment is about all you get nowadays to let a reflection take shape in: ironically, Westerners suspect they will cease to exist if they stop talking for more than a few seconds, to themselves or others. So the artist is caught in a particular bind: while the imagination may bloom best in an attentive stillness, it needs to be seeded in the noisy world. You can't just sit about alone in an old crofter's cottage by a deserted loch, listening to the wind, for instance, pulled into nothingness, and expect to fall pregnant with a novel. A poem or two perhaps, but not much more. Unless, of course, like a Carmelite nun, you think God might come and settle into your emptiness. (For the atheist José Saramago, the Portuguese novelist, God *was* silence: 'God is the silence of the universe,' he wrote in *The Notebook*, 'and man is the cry that gives meaning to this silence.' I find the first part of this statement as hard to make sense of as 'There is no God but God.' Perhaps he was being poetic.)

Noise has its champions, it's only fair to mention. Edward, for instance, the Cambridge scholar in E. M. Forster's story 'Ansell', suddenly tongue-tied while trying to make conversation with the gamekeeper, is panicked by the 'dead silence': to 'educated people,' he says, 'silence matters: it is a token of stupidity and lack of invention. I racked my brains for some remark that would serve to keep my self-respect, but could find none.' The gamekeeper, being uneducated, was perfectly at peace: he thought that silence 'merely meant that neither of us had any more to say'. In *A Passage to India* Forster's picnickers at the Marabar Caves sense a different kind of silence, a 'spiritual silence which invaded more senses than the ear. Life went on as usual, but had no consequences, that is to say, sounds did not echo or thoughts develop.' As a rule, spiritual silences of this kind do not last very long. They leave educated people, such as the picnickers, feeling out of sorts.

Seneca wasn't panicked by silence, but, living above a Roman bathhouse, could not for the life of him 'see that quiet is as necessary to a person who has shut himself away to do some studying as it is usually thought to be'. As he sat upstairs writing, Seneca could hear not just the sound of carpenters sawing, the horn-tuner tuning his horns and the cries of the men hawking drinks and sausages in the street outside, but the grunts of the weightlifters in the bathhouse below, the slap of the masseur's hands on oiled flesh, the splashing in the pools and the shrieks of customers having their armpits plucked. Yet in the midst of this racket, he wrote on 'serenely' (his word). He was, after all, a Stoic. 'If we have turned away from the surface show,' he said, 'then . . . nothing will distract us. Men and birds together in full chorus will never break into our thinking when that thinking is good and has at last come to be of a sure and steady character.' I am impressed.

Thinking is just one of the things people do in hushed seclusion, I know. Some relish moments of stillness for the freedom they offer *from* thought. 'At last,' they think to themselves, 'I can take a break from thinking – and just feel.' But the artist needs to think as well. And, unlike Seneca, most artists can't do it without at least an hour or two of quiet to do it in. Unlike Seneca, most artists need a tower.

And so, some time ago in my tower, I fell to reflecting on noise and silence – especially in a writer's life – and wrote a few words on wordlessness. In a brief lull in the hubbub at one of those writers' festivals we mill about at nowadays, I shared my ruminations with a slightly restless audience hungering, I now suspect, for something more sensational.

On Noise and Silence

O bright, bright,
O bright, bright, bright,
O bright, bright,
Bright, O bright, bright,
Bright, O bright moon.

This is a very old Japanese poem I came across recently, written by a priest who lived about eight hundred years ago and cut off his right ear. In Japanese it's even worse, or perhaps infinitely better, or possibly just different. In Japanese it sounds something like this:

Aka aka ya
Aka aka aka ya
Aka aka . . .
(and so on, ending in)
tsuki
(which is 'moon').

For some of us this sounds as meaningless in either language as the thump of one of those *shishi odoshi* – those ladle-like, bamboo deer-scarers you can still see in streams in Japanese gardens. Fill-empty-clack, fill-empty-clack, fill-empty-clack . . . forever, until time itself bends and snaps.

Others of us may feel zenly transported by it. Indeed, we may feel that we've turned into moon-minds ourselves, as the poet-priest apparently did, walking at night to the prayer hall to meditate. For him, the moon and moon-mindedness were much the same thing. Through the worn words 'bright' and 'moon', as smooth as wood, some of us may have caught the gleam of something, like black lacquer through red on a treasured table-top.

> O bright, bright,
> O bright, bright, bright,
> O bright, bright,
> Bright, O bright, bright,
> Bright, O bright moon.

What I think is that the priest, Myoe the Dreamkeeper, was writing as close to the edge of silence as was possible for a writer to do (without sinking into mindlessness, either silent or cacophonous). But the silence Myoe was edging towards was not silence in quite our Western sense of emptiness – soundlessness, a blank. It was silence in a rather more Japanese sense (naturally enough) which I don't fully understand, but would rather like to.

I would like to because I suspect that this thirteenth-century priest and I (however unlikely this may seem, given what a talker I am, how publicly in love with language) have something in common: coming from different directions, we converge in the desire to transcend the humdrumness of life, with an eye to both the pity of it and to its beauty. (The Japanese express it more confrontingly: Myoe was concerned to make the normal supernormal.) This just means being instead of performing or demanding attention. This is difficult to do if you believe, as we tend to in the West, that being *is* performance. It is particularly hard to do if you are a writer.

Also, as it happens, and this is germane, we have both written out of a tea-consciousness, rather than a wine-consciousness, he his dream diaries, and I my memoirs, although I don't always call them that. Tea-consciousness is refreshed reflection, rather than excitement or inebriation. It's not important whether you drink the finest *pu erh*, say, or Lipton's teabag tea, it's a matter of the colouring of your consciousness. Tea-consciousness draws its strength from the browns and greens deep inside you, wine-consciousness more from the outside, from celebration, friendship and neighbourly feelings. Drifting into tea-consciousness you cohere into something. Drifting into wine-consciousness, you revel in incoherence and the thrill of flux. Perhaps you need both – one-sidedness, as Jung remarked, being the sign of the barbarian – but, being a Puritan at heart, although not necessarily a puritan, I mostly have only tea-consciousness. An archer drinks tea.

So, while I am no Japanese monk, I would like to understand what sort of silence Myoe was edging towards when he wrote, what sort of balance he lit upon between noise and silence. In the opening lines of *Twilight of Love*, a book I wrote about Turgenev and the eclipse of romantic love, this is how I edged towards silence:

> '*Meine Damen und Herren, in wenigen Minuten erreichen wir Baden-Baden.*' Gently braking. 'Ladies

and gentlemen, next stop—' BADEN-BADEN.
Gliding into the station. BADEN-BADEN. Snack-
bar. Lady with lapdog. Hardly a soul about. A Hugo
Boss billboard sliding by. BADEN-BADEN. The hills
to the east hazy, heating up. Paragliders – one, two,
three. Boss again – so sleek. Another brief glimpse
of the blue-green hills. We jolt to a standstill with a
screech. I stare at the sign on the platform outside.
BADEN-BADEN.

Tea, you see, not wine. Or, if you prefer, butoh, not rap. My lines are no haiku, teetering on the edge of silence – I'm too Western for that – but there is an encroaching hush towards the end of my fill-empty-clack, fill-empty-clack, as the train comes to a halt and the eye takes over from the ear, that you can feel in advance promises to be full, not empty – or empty only in a full sense, like silence in the Australian bush, which can be almost ear-splitting if you have the ears to hear, or the silence of an uneventful day of steady drizzle. The lines I've quoted are from the beginning of *Twilight of Love*, but almost everything I've written, now I come to think about it, however noisily it begins (a Cairo café, a Rome railway station, the casbah in Algiers) at least ends with a kind of silent fullness, a coming home, a cohering that a Jungian might call individuation. It's what happens to Lavretsky, the hero of Turgenev's *Nest of Gentlefolk*; after his marriage goes awry: he 'comes home to silence' back on his estate 'as if to the bottom of a river'. He stands gazing out of the window at his garden where 'nothing, hardly even a bumblebee or gnat was stirring . . . listening to the quiet . . . expecting nothing – yet at the same time as if in a state of constant expectation'. Exactly. A silence that's full.

Myoe the priest approached silence not just serenely but (at least in my imagination) joyfully, escaping humdrumness by being piercingly at one with the utterly ordinary. He could do that because he was not afraid of nothingness. For him there could be no such thing as nought. Emptiness for him was a lack of self, not a void. Silence for him, I suspect, was more like the silence you hear after the last note of a symphony has sounded, before the applause begins, or the silence before the needle hits the spinning record.

Eight hundred years later in the nihilistic West, however, the prospect of nothingness – of no-self – throws us into existential panic. The humdrum and banal strike us as harbingers of non-existence. It's as if we feared that unless we ceased noisily performing we might actually cease to be. Reflective inwardness of any kind – even peacefully knitting nowadays – seems fraught with hints of madness. So we tend to babble – at speed. We worship loudly at the shrine of chaos and noise. As artists we come up with loud answers to nothingness: feverish plots, outlandish characters, cataclysmic events, all flying apart at the speed of light. We try to out-talk language (as Susan Sontag put it) and out-music music, out-paint painting. We even babble about babble, swooping about gaudily in the language-clogged air, chattering and gossiping about our own babble, hardly anchored at all any more in just *being* because we can't imagine any longer what that might mean. (Being, as I said, for us *is* performance.) Fill in the blank space – the canvas, the stage, the airwaves, the pages, the screen, even the sides of trams – fill it all in, fill it with anything, just fill it. Embrace cacophony. Hallucinate. Laugh a lot, like the panellists on *Spicks and Specks*. And, as you ride the cosmic big dipper, hold on like grim death to the thought there is either something (and this is it – me being me) or else there is nothing. At least it won't be humdrum.

Tiring of babble, however, but believing they must choose between babble and silence, a few Western writers have chosen silence. If not this, then that. Literally all or nothing. It's a difficult gesture to carry off – almost regal. 'The audience is over,' these eccentrics seem to be saying (to their audience), 'you may go.' It never really works: the prolific novelist Jenny Diski wrote a book called *On Trying to Keep Still*, in which she darted chattily about the world from New Zealand to Somerset and northern Sweden, fearing 'a mad, skittering nothingness ... a fretful pacing in my cage'. She had a small epiphany one night in Lapland – it was night twenty-four hours a day in Lapland while she was there – feeling 'as if I had just been born', but she knew it wouldn't last and it didn't. Another prolific novelist, Sarah Maitland, converted to Roman Catholicism, mistook herself for a nun and ended up reading and talking to herself for hours a day – or to God, as she would see it – in some isolated spot in Scotland. She has written a densely argued, immensely wordy and in places riveting book about it: *A Book of Silence*. I think she might still be in her hideaway. Whether her kind of silence can produce narrative, though, is unclear. Hermits are not well known for their novels and plays. Total silence, God-filled or not, does not produce storytelling.

I wonder if there might be a more interesting way (at least for some of us) to transcend the humdrum, avoiding both the noise and nothingness – the sort of way my Japanese monk Myoe, I imagine, was closing in on. This would be art that was less about itself – less about a frenzied struggle to talk oneself into existence, however temporarily – and more about being transparent. Artful, of course, but revealing, evocative, provocative, regenerative of something fundamental to the reader, so that the reader, the writer, the language and what was being written about would have fewer barriers between them, like the moon and moon-mindedness. Artfulness that turned the normal into the supernormal. Something more like a Flemish interior. Or a celadon plate: so blissfully empty, and at the same time so miraculously, so solidly full – the sky on earth, as it has been called. Blue-jade perfection. Or do I mean imperfection?

Up in my writing room, of a morning, I drink tea from a fake celadon beaker I bought years ago in Japan. (The secret of making real celadon was lost centuries ago.) It is a moment of great delicacy in my day. That the celadon is fake strikes just the right note of imperfection, I think, to needle me into writing something – or at least into thinking something, skirting empty silence warily as I might a snoozing dog.

⌒

Speaking of dogs – I'm back in my tower now – everything comes together in a dog, I find. A new one has just come to live with us. A slim, brown mutt. I really don't think that everything comes together in a cat.

From the day Polly arrived, so thin and skittish and eager to please, straight from a cage at the pound, she made our house feel bigger, like the houses in those dreams in which you suddenly find an attic or a basement that you never knew was there. Like a kaleidoscope, or even a poet, she reconfigured all the random shards of our everyday existence and made them shine. Truly, like a poet, albeit a tongue-tied one. That's what a dog does. She is a bright focus for a whole household. (A cat is never that.

For a life, perhaps, but not a household.) A dog reshapes things, using lots of repetitious motifs. Fiercely present, she somehow makes every unremarkable thing remarkable again: blowflies, hang-gliders, puddles, stacking the dishwasher, peeling a banana. She's out on the back terrace at this very moment, eyeing off a blackbird I'd never have noticed was there.

But it's a paradox: a dog in the house sharpens your sense of being alive – amplifies your very being – yet at the same time is so heartbreakingly mortal. Looking at her now, her eyes, ears and twitching nose trained on that blackbird perched on the edge of the bird-bath, I can't help remembering all the dogs that were once as intensely here with me as she is at this moment, yet now are dead. I remember the feel of their fur, their barks, their quick, warm eyes, their jubilation as I bent to pick up their food bowl . . . Basil the basset's swagger, Max's leaps of joy when I reached for his lead . . . and now nothing. Silence. So many prompts, but all I hear back is silence.

No wonder, in revolt against this silence, so many supernatural tales involve dogs (along with children and all the other untimely dead): we reach out to hold on to them in any way we can because they leave us too soon. We look out for them, we listen out for them, refusing to believe that *everything* we once loved about them has gone. Turgenev has a chilling story about a spectral dog, for example, as does Conan Doyle, of course, but these are just nineteenth-century echoes of medieval tales of hounds from hell, faerie dogs, guardian dogs protecting lonely travellers, churchyard grims and other supernatural canines. More interesting to me is the number of stories of real dogs with supernatural powers, such as Thomas Hardy's dog Wessex. Whenever Hardy's friend Henry Watkins came to visit, Wessex would rush to meet him with joyful barks, although on the whole he was a difficult, snobbish dog with a vicious aversion to postmen in particular. But Wessex had a talent for telepathy. One day when Watkins arrived, his barks turned to troubled whimpering, and he went to sit beside him, pawing at his coat and uttering sharp yaps of distress. It transpired that at that moment Watkins' father was in fact about to die, completely unexpectedly, and (spookier still), when the telephone call came the next morning with the news of his death, Wessex lay quietly with his nose between his paws, although normally he would bark excitedly whenever the telephone rang. Stories such as this one – and they abound, I've had them recounted to me by friends about their own dogs – are a comfort to us because we know that they can only be true if we and our dogs are more than we seem to be: first here, alive, and then zeros.

This must be one of the reasons we love our dogs with such intensity, surely: they are so nakedly and innocently what we've been all along, but pretend not to be. Sally Bowles was right when she sang in *Cabaret* that 'it isn't that long a stay' and dogs remind us of this every day. The brevity of their lives – their short-lived, but euphoric escape from nothingness – is part, as the French writer Roger Grenier puts it, of the very 'hurt of living'. Yet dogs know how to trick time, not fretting about the shortness of their lives. Death has not got them by the throat. Truly, for them (as for Jehovah, not to mention Sally Bowles, once she got in front of the footlights) one day is as a thousand years.

I don't get any of this from a cat. Nor do I get the impression that a cat expects the best from me, as a dog does, even a dog I've just met in the street. This is why I can disappoint a dog, but rarely a cat. It's why a dog can touch me as few cats can. It's not a dog's devotion that disarms me, but the feeling I have that my dog thinks I am good. I can admire a cat, I can be impressed by a cat, even want to stroke a cat, but I am rarely touched. Without even trying, a cat makes me feel second-rate.

Am I blind to something? Undoubtedly. It was out of a moment of play with his cat, according to Sarah Bakewell, a recent biographer, that Montaigne's whole philosophy arose. Perhaps it's like wine-consciousness and tea-consciousness: some of us come alive with dogs and others with cats. I've come across some beautiful songs of praise to cats – for instance, over a thousand years ago an Irish monk in Germany took an hour or two off from translating manuscripts to record this light-hearted tribute to his cat:

> I and Pangur Bán my cat,
> 'Tis a like task that we are at:
> Hunting mice is his delight,
> Hunting words I sit all night.
>
> 'Tis a merry thing to see
> At our tasks how glad are we,
> When at home we sit and find
> Entertainment to our mind.
>
> 'Gainst the wall he sets his eye,
> Full and fierce and sharp and sly;
> 'Gainst the wall of knowledge I
> All my little wisdom try.
>
> So in peace our tasks we ply,
> Pangur Bán my cat and I;

> In our arts we find our bliss,
> I have mine and he has his.

Pangur Bán's presence in this poem is utterly feline: he is the monk's equal companion, a fellow hunter, sociably pursuing his 'art' alongside his friend, the monk. Cat-lovers love to play at companionable equals. There's something of this in a note that Montaigne made about his cat: 'When I play with my cat,' he mused, 'who knows if I am not a pastime to her more than she is to me? . . . We entertain each other with reciprocal monkey tricks. If I have my time to begin or to refuse, so she has hers.'

Every serious cat-lover in the English-speaking world knows at least a few lines from Christopher Smart's *Jubilate Agno* about his cat Jeoffry. A religious poet, Smart was locked up in St Luke's Hospital for Lunatics in 1757 with only Jeoffry for company. Like Pangur Bán, Jeoffry served not his cell-mate (as a dog would do) but a higher master.

> For I will consider my Cat Jeoffry.
> For he is the servant of the Living God duly and
> daily serving him.
> For at the first glance of the glory of God in the East
> he worships in his way.
> For is this done by wreathing his body seven times
> round with elegant quickness.
> For then he leaps up to catch the musk, which is the
> blessing of God
> upon his prayer.
> For he rolls upon prank to work it in.

> For having done duty and received blessing he
> begins to consider himself.

And sharpens his paws, washes himself, fleas himself, rubs himself against a post, 'looks up for his instructions' and then 'goes in quest of food'.

The lord a cat obeys may look, to later poets, more like nature than God. Sarah Day, for instance, evokes this almost out-of-body allegiance in these first lines from her poem 'Cat Bird' about her cat, Mr Grey, who lives just two hills away from where I'm sitting. It begins like this:

> The cat is watching the bird.
> He has taken leave of his body.
> For the moment he has no heartbeat,
> no warmth, no lithe bones
> nor elastic sinew, no tight-sprung energy
> to launch him along a vertical
> or horizontal trajectory.
> He has neither claw nor tail nor teeth,
> he is a laser beam of concentration.
> He is watching the bird and I him.
> He neither hears my voice
> nor feels my footsteps.
> He is a pinpoint.
> Or else he is everything –
> the intricate history of all
> that has brought the two of us
> to this instant.

Given this propensity for obedience to an all-powerful, higher master, it's a wonder that there are no cats in the Bible. (Smart in his madness thought there were.) Perhaps the Jews found cats too blatantly Egyptian. For the Egyptians, cats so aloof, so gracile, just sinew and silk, were virtually divine beings, goddesses in feline form. You could be stoned to death in Egypt for killing a cat. I do not want a goddess in any form about the house. Or even a four-legged equal, whose duty it is to serve some higher, unseen power. I want a dog.

People besotted with their dogs have been writing about their infatuation for several hundred years – ever since dogs became part of the family in early modern Europe, became Blackie and Bonnie and Rex instead of just 'the dog'. J. R. Ackerley, for instance, wrote two books about the German shepherd he'd inherited from a lover who had been carted off to gaol for burglary. When Queenie died in 1961, Ackerley wanted to commit *suttee*. Thomas Mann wrote another classic about a German shepherd, Bashan, in *Bashan and I*. What could I say about dogs that has not been said, not just in these masterpieces, but in dozens of other tributes besides – in Raimond Gaita's *The Philosopher's Dog*, for instance?

What first comes to mind (since I shall try to say something) as I look at Polly eyeballing the blackbird can be bundled up in one little word: fun. Dogs have fun – to make a moment, an hour, a day good, it is enough to have fun. I'm envious because having fun is something I scarcely know how to do. I can't abandon myself to pure amusement, whereas she can. Lying in the sun, chasing other dogs on the beach, eating a bone, smelling a garbage bin – it's all *fun*. Sometimes, just for fun, she will toss a stick in the air and catch it and then do it again. As I watch,

I almost swoon with pleasure. To watch her is bliss. Yet I can't do it myself – I don't know why.

When I was a small child, fun panicked me to the point of seizing up with asthma or, later, doubling up with stomach pains. I don't mean the solitary pleasure of sorting out the stamps in my stamp collection, or even playing Monopoly with my cousins (although that, too, could end badly), but pure, boisterous fun in the backyard with other children – wrestling, hide-and-seek, cowboys and Indians. Is it the complete abandon that I find so threatening? Is it the danger to my self-control? It's not that I am not convivial, but to this day, whenever I see mobs of people 'having fun', I feel my body tighten, my thoughts turn sour, my goodwill become brittle and then dry up. The sight of dogs having fun, on the other hand – gambolling madly with each other, for example, on the beach near our house, yelping with excitement – is like a benediction, a glimpse of another, more intense way of being, like the piercing ecstasy of a show stopper in a Broadway musical – 'Springtime for Hitler and Germany', say, in *The Producers* ('Deutschland is happy and gay'), or 'America' from *West Side Story* or almost anything from *Cabaret*. I revel in it. It yanks me out of my buttoned-up, cramped self. Safe in the dark in my seat in the theatre, I soar with the rest of them.

At the heart of 'fun', according to the etymologists, and certainly of the musical, lies a kernel of volatile thoughts about playing tricks – on reason, good taste, good manners – in a word, on being good. The fun-seeker is a hoaxer, hoaxing time itself and its tyranny. I can't do it, except in the dark at the theatre. Birthday parties, Christmas dinners, rock concerts, Mardi Gras parades, funerals, football finals, carols by candlelight, the mere thought of Mykonos – any kind of celebration, really, especially in a herd – even a game of cards, are all as alien to me as maypole dancing. To a Puritan, it all smacks of mummery and the Whore of Babylon. Wine-consciousness, you see, run riot. ('Come taste the wine,' Minelli sings, 'come hear the band,/Come blow your horn, start celebrating,/Right this way your table's waiting' – all the things I hold myself aloof from in life, but surrender to deliciously in a darkened theatre.)

The Puritan also abominates any lurch towards the irrational. Puritans, at least officially, abominate a lot of things, but particularly unreason. What if two plus two made five? Dostoyevsky's Underground Man asked, and I've never forgotten how that made me sit up straight with alarm when I first read it as a teenager. 'I admit,' he said, 'that two times two makes four is an excellent thing, but if we are to give everything its due, two times two makes five is sometimes a very charming thing as well.' No, it isn't, I shout back, a little peevishly, especially if the mindless mob takes to the idea, which it's bound to – certain postmodernists already have. In *Nineteen Eighty-Four* $2 + 2 = 5$ is state policy instituted to keep the mob mindless. Only in the theatre, seen from a reserved seat, can unreason seduce. Is life a cabaret? No, it's mostly 'four sordid rooms in Chelsea', but for two enchanted hours, *inspirited* to the point of bliss by Joel Grey singing '*Willkommen, bienvenue*, welcome', it seems to be. I want that song to stop now before I explode into a thousand pieces, I want it to go on forever.

The second thing I could say about dogs in my life can also be summed up in a single word: smells. They listen, they watch, they love to be touched, but above all their being is concentrated in their quivering noses. Nothing prissy, no perfumer's transports of delight over the shimmering amber tones of this scent or the orange-blossom-sweet-myrrh accord of another: the world itself is a symphony of smells for them and they are, so to speak, all ears. It's their sense of smell that anchors them in a particular place at a particular hour. My inclination, as a civilised man, is to ignore my nose, except in lifts. Some years ago I talked about my thoughts on noses on ABC radio – noses and the places smells evoke for me, to be precise.

On the Nose

In 'The Nose' Gogol has a civil servant's nose leave his face, become a State Councillor and take to driving about St Petersburg in a gold-braided uniform with high stand-up collar and chamois trousers, praying in the cathedral, window-shopping and generally conducting itself in an outrageously puffed-up fashion.

Now, I've always loved this story because, in a roundabout way, it strikes a blow for the nose – for sniffing out the essence of a city. Noses need all the applause they can get: no other sense organ is as mocked. 'Lead by the nose', 'pay through the nose', 'stick your nose into somebody's business', 'look down your nose at somebody', 'nosey' and so on – eyes and ears, even tongues, get a much more favourable airing. Then there are all those unpleasant nasal words in English starting with 'sn': 'snort', 'snot', 'snuffle', 'snore', 'snoop', 'snooty', 'snicker', 'snivel', even 'snout' – there are dozens of them, all designed to denigrate the nose.

As a rule, we privilege the eyes. We don't fly home from Uluru or Kathmandu and rhapsodise about the smells. Yet (speaking personally) it's the smell of Kathmandu I remember best after all these years – over forty now, since my first visit: a heady blend of dry, grainy aromas (wheat, maize, millet, barley, buckwheat, often roasted, and rice, naturally) together with flowery fragrances and (let's be frank) the faecal. Merely imagining those slow, scented waves of warm odours brings to mind the coloured pictures of me on bicycle, me in temple, me in medieval square. (Not the other way around.) Delacroix, the French Romantic painter, when writing about Marrakech in Morocco, another city I first visited over forty years ago, said not a word about the colour of the sky or the saddle-bags or the robes, luminescent against mud walls, or even the tiled walls of a turquoise that almost knifes into the eye. No, what Delacroix was struck by above all else was 'the perfume of old hay and butter and dust'. He was an amazing colourist for the eye, but, unexpectedly, for the nose as well.

Sadly, both Marrakech and Kathmandu probably smell more or less alike nowadays. I haven't been back for years, but I suspect that large parts of them even look the same. There is one global smell now, blanketing all the world's cities: gasoline. Stick your head out of the window in Sydney or Scunthorpe, Budapest or Broken Hill, and you'll find that the delicate panorama of whiffs and almost undetectable redolences that once gave nasal delight, the vista of reeks and, in pockets, aromas and tangs with here and there a foulness, has been blanketed over, snuffed out, *besouped* (as I'd say) by gasoline. Nowadays to recover our olfactory sight, as it were, we have to leave the city and head for the bush.

There's one small consolation: not all gasolines smell the same. Our basset Basil went crazy with excitement when a taxi drew up in the street outside, for instance, not because he could read the words TAXIS COMBINED on the door, although he *was* smart, but because he could smell the diesel. And taxis meant visitors, and visitors meant attention. Then there's a particular kind of low-grade gasoline that whisks me straight back to Moscow in the mid-sixties – the merest transparent trace of it in the air (I think of it as blunt and brownish) and I'm instantly back there. I can see and hear it all: the fuggy buses and damp coats, the stairwells reeking of failure, smells almost like moans, the strolling couples in the parks in autumn and spring, strumming guitars and slurping at ice-creams, the underground station escalators plunging you into the roaring bowels of the city – it's a Soviet smell. It still wafts through my occasional dreams of being young again, bringing back feelings and kitchens and arguments and those creaking Russian parquet floors and . . . well, there's no end to it, really. All from the tweak of a nostril.

When you know a city well, you can sometimes still plunge nasally beneath the bland petrochemical surface of things to catch the whiff of something aromatically characteristic of a place. Sydney, for me, is a case in point: beneath its suffocating quilt of aviation fuel and related effluvia, I can often still sense its sickly essence: hops, plus the smell of an old handbag left out in the sun.

In the old days, the *je ne sais quoi* of a place often had to do with cigarettes: I'm sure the Soviet fug was also shot through with that mixture of the acrid and sweet, the pungent and spicy, which makes cigarette fumes so evocative of this city or that, or even of this building or that. To me the Lenin Library in Moscow didn't smell of books at all, it smelt of damp scarves, floor polish and cigarettes. At the heart of the library was a smoking room which, as the door swung open, leaked a gooey, leather-coloured odour out into the building. That tawny scent, smeared with wet wool and beeswax, means knowledge to me. Knowledge came with that smell.

Caught trying to flee the country on a false passport, Gogol's nose was finally put back in its place on the face of a civil servant, at the bottom of the sensual hierarchy. In modern society that's pretty much where it still languishes, way behind taste, hearing and sight. No perfumer's masterpiece, not even Chanel No. 5 or Black by Bulgari, will ever be compared with the triumphs of composers or visual artists – a Bach partita or Cézanne's *Pommes et oranges* – or, for that matter, of master chefs. Even the connection between smells and sex can't give the nose status: smells might be sexy, and sex can certainly be smelly, but, all the same, however popular sex is, it remains too animal for its odours to join the higher pleasures. Certain perfumes, it's true, worn in the advertisements by slinky, half-naked women and men like sleepy panthers, still trade on erotic promise, but I doubt that anyone much really falls for it these days. A splash or two of some concoction by Guerlain or Jean Patou before you go out into the night might be sexually bracing, and certainly expensive, but it will never be as seductive as what you see and hear and taste and touch.

When, I wonder, will the refined nose at last be able to hold its head up high in civilised society?

∽

For my dog Polly, whose nose is almost inconceivably refined (her olfactory periscope, as it were, is up and swivelling at this very moment), the question never arises.

And there's a third aptitude of hers that I envy as well: idleness. Across the centuries and across the globe, writers have written in praise of idleness: Seneca, Sei Shōnagon, Montaigne, Johnson, Byron, Lamb, Stevenson, Chesterton, Kenko and many others. Even Jesus, in his Sermon on the Mount, sounded sceptical about the value of work: 'Behold the fowls of the air: for they sow not, neither do they reap, nor gather into barns; yet your heavenly Father feedeth them . . . Consider the lilies of the field, how they grow; they toil not, neither do they spin: and yet I say unto you that even Solomon in all his glory was not arrayed like one of these.' He had a different agenda from the other thinkers on the subject, I know – 'don't be distrustful of God's provision for you' was the message he was hammering that day – but, ironically, what reminded me of Jesus' words was an article quoting him that I googled yesterday by the Marxist writer Paul Lafargue. (Marx said that if Lafargue was a Marxist then he, Marx, wasn't, but Lafargue thought he was and that's good enough for me. And he married Marx's daughter.) 'The Right to be Lazy' is the article's title, and in it Lafargue argues that the 'passion for work' is a delusion, a capitalist plot, supported by 'priests, economists and moralists', to 'cast a sacred halo over work', thereby enslaving the proletariat and exhausting its 'vital forces' to the enrichment of the leisured ruling class. These days the ruling class itself seems to share the delusion.

Yet far more thinkers, starting with Plutarch, have written against idleness. And however strong my suspicion is that idleness is the key to a well-lived life – to keeping one's 'vital forces' intact – I find it hard to ease myself into it.

Indolence, needless to say, with its connotations of sluggishness and (worse) drowsiness, is anathema, but idleness, while it may look like indolence to the casual observer, has little in common with it. Indeed, grasping the difference between the two is surely crucial to succeeding in living well. The idler can be pure attention (while reading, thinking, talking, roaming, listening to music), whereas indolence is pure sloth.

Polly was born guiltlessly idle, being a dog. At this precise moment, it's true, she's involved in a major project, sniffing for rats around the compost bins, but by nature she is idle. Like most Westerners, however, I have had to learn how to be idle, and I began learning far too late. I didn't 'bail out', as Sarah Bakewell says of Montaigne's decision to stop being busy, until I was fifty. (Montaigne retired at thirty-seven – but then he had a castle and vineyards in Gascony to fall back on.) I only mention Montaigne because I like the expression 'bail out', although admittedly the master essayist in his tower is never far from my mind at the moment. And 'bail out' reminds me of a nautical phrase Seneca used in his advice to his friend Serenus who was having trouble adjusting to retirement: he wrote of the need to lower our sails – or at least of the danger of letting out 'a great amount of sail' – if we want to avoid being shipwrecked on our voyage through life. Mindful tranquillity, Seneca warns, can take a long time to become a habit – in fact, your first attempts at it might even cause considerable distress. Or, as Montaigne put it, when idleness first begins to settle, now and again your mind might even bolt in fright like a runaway horse.

When you first let your sails drop, Seneca tells Serenus, unless you have deep self-knowledge, you can find yourself panicked by the lack of outward activity. In fact, you can feel almost 'seasick' with anxiety. Sounding extraordinarily modern, Seneca writes about the temptation for the man (he disregarded women – he wasn't *that* modern) who has not cultivated a settled mind to rush about the world, seeking now a more temperate climate, some Roman Noosa, now a desert, as I've just done in Syria, now city life with its marketplaces, crowds and entertainments. You can become sick with a kind of 'restless inactivity', first lapsing into sluggishness and torpor, he says, then rushing pointlessly to see a fire. It's the all-or-nothing syndrome again. Yet if you do try to find consolation in the fluctuations of your own thoughts, you may well be accused of being wrapped up in yourself and being boring. The retreat from busyness into focused tranquillity must, as Seneca warned Serenus, be gradual or you might go mad.

The aptitude for idleness, I am convinced, lies at the heart of another art that needs robust defence in our times: the art of good conversation, conversation that shivers like sheet lightning in summer. After all, at every level, from disarmament negotiations to coping with domestic tensions, dialogue is the key to sanity – even to goodness, I suspect, to give Dostoyevsky his due (since his fictions are the embodiment of it). It's much better to let the devil deep inside you have his say in a vigorous exchange than to turn into his puppet.

The biblical God comes across as addicted to the monologue, it must be said, and this is one of the reasons that being good for Him is so uninteresting. Being good in monologic fashion is not just monotonous, though, like sitting in church, but dangerous: monologue leads to lunacy and death. Yet, instead of dialogue, what we resort to is debate, which is just monologue with two faces. True conversation links 'I's' – fully fledged I's, comfortable with other I's – which is why women are so good at it, I think.

Elated by reading Stephen Miller's *Conversation*, one of many recent discussions of its history and uncertain future, I went onto the airwaves in what the *Australian* newspaper calls 'the alternative universe of Radio National' to talk about what I had discovered.

Conversation

'The grand business of our lives,' the novelist Henry Fielding said, 'the foundation of everything, either useful or pleasant' is conversation. It's quite a claim. His contemporary Samuel Johnson was hardly less emphatic: 'There is in this world,' he said, 'no real delight (excepting those of sensuality) but the exchange of ideas in conversation.' They were eighteenth-century English gentlemen, so their enthusiasm is not surprising: the eighteenth century was the heyday of conversation in England, and some would say in France as well.

In France we associate conversation with the *salon*, those gatherings of wits and thinkers in the drawing rooms (originally the bedrooms) of cultivated Parisian hostesses such as Madame Geoffrin, Sophie de Condorcet and Madame du Deffand (Horace Walpole's friend). A *salon* was no mere book group. In the best drawing rooms, disparate intellects 'fell into harmony like the strings of an instrument touched by an able hand', in the words of the *encyclopédiste* Marmontel, a regular at one of the most celebrated.

In England conversation flourished more in the men's clubs and the dining rooms of the well-to-do (although English *salons* did exist) and, above all, in the coffee houses, there being some two thousand coffee houses in London in the mid-eighteenth century. Some gentlemen – not *quite* so many ladies – spent the whole morning reading the newspapers and conversing in these 'seminaries of sedition', as the High Church Tories called them.

I doubt that many of us would echo Fielding's or Johnson's comments nowadays. Conversation 'the foundation of everything'? Hardly. Did they have in mind an art we've for some reason lost? Was it perhaps something you had to have leisure and servants to be able to cultivate and enjoy?

It's tempting to think to ourselves when we read about the pleasures of lively conversation in earlier times at Will's Coffee House in London, say, where you might have heard Dryden holding forth, or at Garraway's (a favourite of Pepys') or the Rainbow (David Hume was a regular there): it's never like that at Starbucks – or even at that smart new place we went to last Sunday with the overpriced Camargue red rice salad and rude waiters. Never.

And when we read of Virginia Woolf popping into Lady Ottoline's with Rupert Brooke and being swept up in a whirlpool of scintillating gossip – Augustus John holding forth in one corner, Bertie Russell by the window, Churchill darting in and out of the fray on his way to see the king (and sparks flew, apparently; the conversation *crackled*) – we can't help thinking that it's never quite like that for us when we drop in to see *anybody*. Nowadays people either mutter incoherently like Wyatt Earp, their eyes glued to the display on their mobiles, or else they shout at you like North

Korean newsreaders, taking it in turns to declaim. When it comes to conversation, something seems to have gone badly awry.

Yet really we shouldn't think like that. Yes, some things no doubt have changed for the worse, but, apart from anything else, many minds quite as thrilling as Samuel Johnson's, Virginia Woolf's or Bertrand Russell's have had deep reservations about conversation for centuries. The ancient Hebrews don't seem to have put much value on it, for a start – at least, there's precious little conversation in the Bible, which is one long harangue, really: do this, do that, be quiet while I issue a proclamation. And, even though the ancient Athenians were *supposed* to be great talkers (at least compared to the laconic Spartans), the ancient texts tend not to include exchanges we'd nowadays call 'conversations'. Perhaps on a fine morning in the agora in Athens it was different – surely it must have been.

Closer to our own time, Jean-Jacques Rousseau considered conversation frivolous. He could only seriously love mankind by living well away from it. Finding sociability irksome, and doubtful, it seems sometimes, about whether or not other I's actually existed, he preferred solitary walks in beautiful surroundings and reverie (too effeminate an occupation for our tastes these days). Romanticism turned out to be good for letter-writing, declarations and soliloquies, but not for conversation. Thomas Gray, the poet, preferred lonely crags and sublime prospects to coffee houses, especially in the Scottish Highlands, where conversation – many have testified to this – was almost non-existent. Presbyterianism has never been good for animated intercourse.

A little later, Thomas de Quincey was also disdainful of conversation, at least when he was young. He spoke rather eloquently of 'caring as little what absurdities men practised in their vast tennis-courts of conversation, where the ball is flying backwards and forwards to no purpose for ever, as what tricks Englishmen might play with the monstrous national debt'. Across the Atlantic, Thoreau believed that conversation made people superficial because it undermined their appreciation of Nature (which is not the same as nature). You sort of know what these men meant (in their different ways) – solitude, especially in the bosom of Nature (a forest, a desert, an ocean) can give such amplitude to your thoughts and feelings that any kind of human utterance seems shallow, even pointless, by comparison. But few of us can live like that all the time. And if we're going to live amongst other people, then our conversations with them may as well be *good* ones – pleasurable, at times enriching, refining our sensibilities, refreshing our spirits.

But what exactly is 'good conversation'? Before we get too glum about whether or not conversation is in decline – at least in the Western world – we should first make sure we know what we mean by '*good* conversation'. There are scores of books on the subject – hundreds, probably – after all, Cicero was writing about it two thousand years ago and those with the leisure to indulge in it have been discussing it ever since. Reading a couple of the latest offerings (Theodore Zeldin's *Conversation: how talk can change your life* and Stephen Miller's recent *Conversation: a history of a declining art*), I couldn't help feeling that what 'good conversation' is thought to be still depends very much on who's doing the thinking – and when and where. What I thought several decades ago as a student in Canberra living with other students is not at all what I think as a middle-aged man in the Hobart suburbs.

There's consensus on a few things, though. For example, it's widely agreed that a conversation is an exchange, but not of announcements, monologues or even arguments. As opposed to idle chitchat, conversation is an exchange of ideas, insights, information and feelings that changes the participants. So it's like a fire, a fire that spreads horizontally, refining, reshaping, even scorching and rekindling everyone present as it goes.

When I say that the fire spreads horizontally, I mean that, although those catching fire may not be equal in wealth, understanding or social status, they must feel as if, for the duration of the conversation, they are on the same plane. Which is why zealots and counsellors are generally not good at it.

In *Arabesques*, the memoir I published not so long ago, there's a character called Albert, a Frenchman from Pondicherry, an octogenarian, who shares this slightly old-fashioned view of conversation. It can be bamboozling for the young, who no longer have (or do not yet have) the art, and Albert himself can get preachy when the subject turns to Eastern religions (which have a hold on him), but

> Albert wanted to talk. More than that, he wanted a conversation. For Albert a conversation is chiefly a game of skill. Nothing raises his spirits more than a good-natured, lively jousting-match with friends. A bit of gossip, a touch of banter, together with a vigorous exchange of opinions on whatever subject comes to hand. Albert would have felt right at home in one of those eighteenth-century London coffee houses frequented by Swift or Johnson.
>
> You can forget as he swirls about in conversation that movement of any kind these days is difficult for him. And he won't put up with what he calls '*les*

futilités' – airy-fairy claptrap of any kind. He likes you to speak from your own experience, not repeat something somebody else has said or written. In fact, I'm sure I've even heard him quote Gide on the subject: 'It's not enough for me to *read* that the sands on the beach are soft, I want my bare feet to feel it.' Generally, however, he makes his point with mangoes. 'Mangoes,' he is much given to saying, once you get him started on almost any subject – Sanskrit poetry, St Augustine, Pondicherry, anything, really – 'have a taste that can't be imagined by anyone who hasn't eaten one.' Then, seizing the high ground, he generally goes on: 'A mango-lover can explain the taste in terms of melons or papayas, but in the end words will fail him. If you want to know what a mango tastes like, you have to taste one yourself.' What Albert means is that words will fail *you*, not him, in this discussion of things he has tasted many times. Clearly relishing the silence his mention of mangoes always produces, if only momentarily, he usually takes a sip of tea at this point (his years in Pondicherry mean that there's always a pot of it within reach) and sits back waiting for you to make the next ill-advised move. He has a softer side, but, on the whole, he likes to keep you on your toes.

So when he finally asked me, while clearing away the remains of the curried fish that first evening, what I was doing in the south of France this time, and Daniel said, a little too quickly, that I

was there to 'play hide-and-seek with André Gide',
I wasn't too surprised to hear him say: 'I met him
once, you know.'

Good conversation is generally informal, as it is *chez* Albert – it's a matter of spontaneous combustion, so to speak – although the word has been used to describe semi-formal gatherings as well, as in the *salons*: when Boswell said, 'I was at a conversation at Langton's,' he meant something closer to what is nowadays called in English a *conversazione* – an exchange that is not exactly choreographed, but set up in some way. 'Yesterday I had a conversazione,' Hester Thrale (who ran her own *salon*) wrote to Fanny Burney in 1781. 'Mrs Montagu was brilliant in diamonds,' she went on, 'solid in judgment, critical in talk ... Johnson was good-humoured, Lord John Cointon attentive, Dr Bowdler lame, and my master not asleep.'

Perhaps, at its best, the modern book group is an example of the *conversazione*. In the United States there are now networks such as the Conversation Café network and the Socrates Café which apparently organise conversations in this semi-formal way.

Now, here's where it gets interesting: Stephen Miller is very insistent that one of conversation's essential qualities is what I might call urbanity – politeness, if you like, being disposed to please your companions, refraining from violent outbursts, anything that would bore, stifle or anger anyone present. Over 400 centuries ago, Montaigne, a dazzling conversationalist, put it like this: 'If there is anyone, any good fellowship of men in town or country, in France or elsewhere, whom my frame of mind pleases and whose frame of mind pleases me, they have but to whistle through their fingers and I'll come and furnish them with "essays" in flesh and blood.' Swift, too, believed that good conversation was a matter of good manners. It was, he said, 'the art of making every reasonable person in the company easy' – that's why he thought that women were ideally always present: they restrained men's natural tendency to become vicious.

But isn't there something rather suspicious, even prissy, about unfailing good manners? Aren't they often hypocritical, a cover for toadyism and worse? What about honesty and passion and the frank expression of strongly held beliefs? Aren't these all good things? (Personally, I value clearly held beliefs over strongly held ones, but I suspect I'm in a minority.) Well, yes, they are, especially for clearing the air or televised debates, but they're not necessarily good for conversation. Good conversation is more like friendship: it works best between people who share basic values, if not beliefs, and whose politeness towards one another is the honest expression of regard for each other's feelings. Like friendship, it thrives not on anger or one-upmanship, but on (and here's an old-fashioned word, but there's no other) raillery. Three hundred years ago Swift said that raillery was the 'finest part of conversation', yet to this day it's widely misunderstood, mistaken for sarcasm, confused with repartee, or seen as a sign of cruelty or arrogance. Perhaps we imagine it's connected to railing. On the contrary, raillery is everything that railing is not: it's light-hearted criticism, it's close to banter, it's play, it's teasing, it's joshing, it makes you smile and even laugh. It's the spice that leavens the lump of blandness that courtesy might smother a conversation (or friendship) with.

I wonder how many people these days even know what the word 'raillery' means. Pessimists might see this as just one more sign of the decline of conversation in the modern world. 'You see?'

they would say (and Stephen Miller would nod in agreement). We're mired in a 'let it all hang out' ethos these days, which *sounds* like a good idea – or it did in the 1960s – so honest, so authentic, so real, yet all it amounts to, as often as not, is 'I'll say what I think and, if you don't like it, you can get stuffed.' (Miller puts it even more bluntly.) However, this kind of angry narcissism, worn like a badge of honour by all the grunters, mumblers, ranters and ravers of popular culture, locked in an endless loop of self-reflection, actually kills good conversation.

Miller sees a society, particularly in the United States, almost entirely given over to what he calls 'conversation avoidance techniques' of various kinds: video games, television chat shows, text-messaging, self-obsessed blogging, and academic disciplines so specialised that only a handful of men and women in the universe can talk about them to each other. To him it's almost as if whole swathes of Western society have become autistic.

America didn't need mobile phones and academic specialisation, however, to become infertile ground for conversation. A number of foreigners in the nineteenth century claimed that conversation was not to be had in America at all, except perhaps in Boston, where there were excellent clubs. Mrs Trollope, Dickens, Alexis de Tocqueville and Henry James all commented on the inability of American men to do anything except talk business and spit, and of American women to do much more than quote the Bible at each other. A couple of generations later that incarnation of American masculinity Ernest Hemingway was asserting that conversation was a kind of 'whistling in the dark' – meaningless and banal. Real men, it seems, did not indulge. Indeed, if you saw *Brokeback Mountain*, you'll have noticed that, whatever sort of un-Hemingway-like behaviour real American men might now permit themselves (so long as it ends badly), conversation still causes them acute embarrassment. The women in the film chatter, rather than converse, driving the men mad, while the men . . . Well, you'd have to see the movie, really.

On the whole I'm not as pessimistic about conversation as Stephen Miller, unless I've just been travelling on a Hobart bus. I think it's probably always been a rare art – *good* conversation, that is. It may well have flourished in London's coffee houses three hundred years ago, or in the *salons* of Paris, or on the back verandahs and in the living rooms of memory . . . In that kindlier world before television and its so-called chat shows, before text-messaging, computer games and all the other excuses we have for not conversing came along. But I suspect that for most people conversation, as opposed to mere talk, or the giving of advice, or sounding off, or sermonising, or trying to impress, has always been too delicate, too demanding a skill to have been widely practised.

As Theodore Zeldin writes, 'creating equal conversations is now the supreme art'. Mastering it is not compulsory, billions of people get on perfectly well thinking it's what Oprah Winfrey does, but if you want to turn your own life into an individual work of art – and why not? – then it's worth working at.

∽

Perhaps that's aiming too high.

Now, the art of conversation (and, indeed, friendship, finally trashed by Facebook) is vital, I am convinced, to another vanishing art: the essayist's – or at least to the art of the personal essay. At one level this peculiar genre is sought after by readers with renewed vigour in our times, as is memoir, with Montaigne's name now popping up everywhere – well, not in any university classrooms, obviously, let alone in the popular press or on television chat shows, but wherever writers can count on their readers' taste and education. (If this sounds elitist, I make no apology: there's a reward for being educated.) It's remarkable, really, given that Montaigne was French, has been dead for over four hundred years and only wrote one book – two if you count his travel journals. Not everyone is enamoured of him: for instance, the contemporary French writer Charles Dantzig (novelist, poet, essayist) says that he finds Montaigne 'frivolous' and 'a bloody pain in the neck'. But the audience for what Dantzig calls his 'universal gossip-mongering' is undeniably growing. In other words, there seems to be a small rebellion underway: it's as if a few subversives have decided to take a stand against the replacement of attentive tranquillity by chatter in our society. At another level, though, the battle for the personal essay to be noticed seems already lost. This is the era of political commentary, polemics on social issues, the review, the personal rant, the tweet and talk-of-the-town columns.

Bearing all this in mind, in 2010 I flew the flag for the personal essay (as well as conversation, idleness, dogs and other *idées fixes* of mine) at a symposium at the National Library of Australia held to mark the awarding of the Calibre essay prizes. The event went under the cleverly Montaignesque title of 'Essaying'. I did my best to sound upbeat.

Letters to an Unknown Friend

What a wonderful thing is the essay! What a hymn to the human mind and its vagaries and cogitations – to its humanness!

To celebrate the essay with this degree of fanfare, to take it as seriously as today's events do, shows a certain amount of chutzpah, I think – of 'courage' in the Sir Humphrey Appleby sense of the word. ('A courageous decision, Minister.')

After all – and I hope you'll allow me to be brutally frank, writing them myself as I do – nobody ever got the Nobel Prize for writing essays. Nobody is likely to say: ah, yes, Virginia Woolf, or Robert Louis Stevenson, what superb essayists they were. No, they talk first about *To the Lighthouse* and *Dr Jekyll and Mr Hyde*. There is something in our culture of the country cousin (of good family, mind, and well spoken, but not quite first-night-at-the-opera) about the essay.

All too often it's thought of as a bit of harmless throat-clearing (smelling of dry almonds, according to one commentator) useful for filling a puzzling silence between novels. A novel, now there's something you can take seriously. A novel is storytelling, which is what culture itself is, really (isn't it?) – plus folk-dancing and cooking. An essay is just commentary. Write a novel or three and they'll soon sit up in Stockholm; a *single* novel in the shops and you could be strutting your stuff at Adelaide Writers' Week in no time – or in Vancouver or Hay-on-Wye. On the other hand, when your publisher asks you what you're working on next and you tell him a book of essays, watch his face fall.

A novel is grand, even if we no longer believe in grand narratives – at least, not officially. Novels have sweep. Essays are so *small*. (As each of *us* is small, of course, when all is said and done, even Seneca or Susan Sontag, not to mention Oprah Winfrey or the Queen, which is why I think that the essay is vital to a civilised life.)

And in turn it's why a book such as Alan Bennett's *An Uncommon Reader* – did you ever read it? It's about the Queen taking to books – is such a joy: she may be grand, but she's also small, like us. But I digress, being an essayist at heart, and that is what we do. Oh, I've *called* a couple of my books 'novels', but deep down I'm just a gossip. In Damien Hirst's words, 'Sometimes I feel I have nothing to say, and that's something I often want to communicate.' It's just a great shame that Hirst chose art as his medium. Or, as the Portuguese writer Fernando Pessoa – or at least a 'mutilated' version of Fernando Pessoa, who had so many selves he called his soul 'a hidden orchestra' – once wrote, 'I sometimes write *because* I feel I have nothing to say.' But perhaps in his case it was all a pose. At least it led to the creation of one of the twentieth century's masterpieces, the inconsolably melancholy drift of reveries called *The Book of Disquiet.*

Georg Lukács even thought that the smallness of the essay – or rather the essayist's need to give up his hopes of bigness while explaining his most profound ideas – the essayist's 'ironic modesty', as he calls it – is essential to its status.

But, but, but, you will object – and I do take your point – there are essays aplenty on grand subjects: on Aboriginal deaths in custody, on global warming, on nuclear non-proliferation, adultery in the French novel and every other matter of consequence you can think of. Of course there are – they're not all about a man chasing his hat or bed-wetting or going out for a walk to buy a pencil – although some of the most memorable have been. And these essays on grand subjects will appear in important newspapers, in the *Times Literary Supplement* and the *New York Review of Books*, and be anthologised in much remarked-upon tomes – and deservedly. And this is good. They need no defence from me. These are the oils in the national gallery.

But what I would like to gossip about today is the standing of the more fugitive form in the twenty-first century – the perfectly judged watercolours, the more personal kind of essay, the sort of thing we write just because we want to tell someone something, something we must find the words for now, before the moment passes.

Montaigne began writing his essays after his much-loved friend Étienne de la Boétie died suddenly and he needed someone to talk to. So he talked to his unknown friend, his reader – wrote letters to *him*. About anything that came into his mind, really – and a lot of things did (friendship, drunkenness, cannibals, Heracleitus, prayer, kidney stones and so on), often in Latin, his first language – or so we're told. (I find it hard to *quite* believe it – in rural Gascony in the 1530s, with only his tutor to talk to, but we're assured it's true.) It's the intimacy with *me*, whom he doesn't know, that still astonishes and disarms. Nowadays, when the vast bulk of the population never seems to stop talking and being talked at – on public conveyances, at home, in the office, even face to face, if pressed – nowadays Montaigne's predicament when La Boétie died is almost unimaginable. Yet these days our intimacy is faux. I read last week that the average American teenage girl (twelve to seventeen) sends eighty text messages a day – that's five every waking hour. And she also phones, emails, tweets and pops on and off Facebook. This is to live out life's banality, not redeem it, as the essayist seeks to do. You may be wondering why Montaigne didn't talk to his wife, whom he married when La Boétie died, *faute de mieux*, but the thought never occurred to him – and would no doubt have left her nonplussed as well. No, no – you talk about the things that matter to an equal, not your wife. And we can be grateful that it was so – we can now imagine ourselves, five hundred years later, as Montaigne's unknown friend and relish the intimacy.

The art of conversation (everyone seems to agree) – the rapidly disappearing art of intimate conversation in this internet-addicted world of ours – is somehow central to the health of the personal essay, the kind I think does need some defence, unlike its more impersonal cousin. Given that for Montaigne – and I quote – conversation was 'at the top of the pyramid of all human activities: above writing and far above reading' (he claimed he'd rather lose his sight than his hearing), you might have expected the essay (of the so-called 'familiar' or personal kind) to flourish in France.

In fact, it first came into its own in its modern form in England, pre-industrial England, and some even believe that is because it grew out of the culture of conversation in London coffee houses in the eighteenth century over newspapers – a culture now seriously under threat. (I'm just back from Melbourne where the cafés are full of people texting, typing on laptops or concentratedly eating, as if *that* were why one went to a café.) Out of these encounters (disputatious often, but friend to friend) grew the essay – friend to unknown friend. Yet now? A friend of mine, for instance, just back from Valparaiso, sent me a brief email recently: 'Just been to Valparaiso. You'd love it. See my blog.' 'No,' I wrote back, a little too testily perhaps (but essayists are often testy, it's part of being an essayist as opposed to being a poet or novelist). 'No,' I said, 'I won't see your blog. I am not interested in Valparaiso, I am interested in having a chat with you – just you and me – even about Valparaiso, if you wish. I am interested in the chat. Or write it up for *The Monthly* – I am also interested in transfiguration.' Relations have cooled. But I won't read his blog. Valparaiso, like Montaigne's cannibals, is quite beside the point.

Although coffee houses and clubs went into a decline eventually, like the newspapers, something had taken root in England, something that gave rise to Lamb and Hazlitt and Chesterton and Orwell and Virginia Woolf and numerous others: a taste for polished company. Essayists went all formal during the Victorian era, it's true, but then, last century, returned to a quirkier, more self-revealing form with a sigh of relief.

But it's not just the second-class status and ill-health of the conversational core of the essay (and the personal essay in particular) that make me wonder if it's quite suited to our times. Of course, as an essayist of sorts, I *would* say that, because traditionally essayists have tended to bemoan something, frequently looking to the past and resisting the idea of being up-to-date. Let me quote Charles Lamb, for instance, who spoke of his 'tender regret' for the passing of things in his essay on New Year's Eve:

> I am naturally, beforehand, shy of novelties;
> new books, new faces, new years – from some
> mental twist which makes it difficult in me to face
> the prospective. I have almost ceased to hope;
> and am sanguine only in the prospects of other
> (former) years. I plunge into foregone visions
> and conclusions. I encounter pell-mell with past
> disappointments . . . I play over again for love, as
> the gamesters phrase it, games, for which I once
> paid so dear.

(I once read Lamb at school in North Sydney, where now I suppose they compare ads for Harvey Norman with ads for Officeworks. It's all text, after all, isn't it?)

But it's not that, either – not just the common tendency of the most celebrated essayist to be slightly behind the times in this frantically up-to-the-minute era – that makes me uncertain about the essay's fate in the years to come. Youth is the current obsession within Western culture – youth may not have power (that's a different matter), but youth is what the spotlight is on, everywhere from *New Idea* and *Marie Claire* to every commercial television channel and David Jones menswear department.

If it's not in the spotlight, it whines like an unruly child until it is. Youth – its fantasies, tastes, diseases, values, fashions, humour, language, obsessions, ambitions and needs – leads the parade on Main Street these days. And why shouldn't it? Youth has hope. There are hopes for it. Historically, however, essays (of the kind I'm talking about) were written by older writers who, like Lamb, had 'almost ceased to hope'. Youth, by and large, has better things to do with its time than write personal essays – it's actually quite hard to think of many widely read essays by young writers – although now and again they may pen formal essays. It probably thinks it also has better things to do with its time than read personal essays: they're too moderate, too on-the-one-hand-this on-the-other-hand-that. Montaigne himself failed to excite the Austrian writer Stefan Zweig, for example, when he was young: 'What appeal could there be for a twenty-year-old youth in the rambling excursus of a Sieur de Montaigne on the "Ceremony of interview of kings" or his "Considerations on Cicero"?' Yet later in life Montaigne became Zweig's 'indispensable helper, confidant and friend'.

It also takes time to come up with the 'soloist's personal signature' (to quote Elizabeth Hardwick) that typically characterises the accomplished essay. It is hard, until you have reached your mature years, to have the sense of a well-integrated self unafraid to embrace its own uncertainties and frailties – its humanness – that essay-writing requires. Not impossible, but hard. As someone or other has observed, the young are better at poetry and mathematics. The older amongst us may sit in their towers like Montaigne and write letters to unknown friends about sumptuary laws, say, or smells or rereading Virgil, but they will do it in the half-light nowadays. It's not their era.

But there's more to it than even that. Without a capacity for idleness – and it is an art, one it's not always practical to cultivate in your younger years, once you've left your childhood behind you – you cannot follow in Montaigne's footsteps.

As is well-established, dogs do it best, having that perfect combination of an unhurried appreciation of the moment and alertness to stabs of narrative – nothing grand – that make for fine essays. (I'm not sure about cats – I think cats very often do confuse idleness with indolence.) A dog has no concept of what 'in toto' means – and nor does an essayist (of the kind I'm talking about). A dog – you can tell by the eyes – has many 'tender regrets'. And I tenderly regret that they can't write essays.

To write about sleep or laughter or riding in coaches, as Montaigne did, you need to know how to be idle. Yet in Australia in the twenty-first century we do not live in a society that values idleness. We value industry – industriousness, productivity, busyness.

'I expect you're very busy,' people say to me sometimes. 'No, not busy at all,' I say. 'Preoccupied, but not busy.' Nobody these days knows how to take in this information – it's like admitting that you detest children.

Here's what Robert Louis Stevenson had to say about busyness:

> Extreme busyness, whether at school or college, kirk or market, is a symptom of deficient vitality; and a faculty for idleness implies a catholic appetite and a strong sense of personal identity. There is a sort of dead-alive, hackneyed people about, who are scarcely conscious of living except in the exercise of some conventional occupation. Bring these fellows into the country, or set them aboard ship, and you will see how they pine for their desk or their study. They have no curiosity; they cannot give themselves over to random provocations . . . they cannot be idle, their nature is not generous enough; and they pass those hours in a sort of coma, which are not dedicated to furious moiling in the gold-mill . . . And it is not by any means certain that a man's business

is the most important thing he has to do. To an impartial estimate it will seem clear that many of the wisest, most virtuous, and most beneficent parts that are to be played upon the Theatre of Life are filled by gratuitous performers, and pass, amongst the world at large, as phases of idleness.

Yet our world not only insists that we be unendingly industrious, it also demands, as never before, that we pay attention to the products of others' industry. 'Pay attention to me!' it shouts at us, ceaselessly. 'Buy me! When you're not working, shop!' In this noisy world of productivity and buying, the essayist is a foreigner. He – or she, but it's traditionally a he – is a rambler – a *flâneur*, sometimes translated as 'idler', if you want to be snooty about it – jotting down for the delectation of his unknown friend a trail of observations on whatever he passes: Cato the Younger, liars, fasting, almost anything. He's wily, of course. His idleness is partly feigned: he's pandering to the leisured aristocrat inside himself, never the peasant – well, Montaigne *was* an aristocrat, but few of us are. He isn't really a 'ranging spaniel', either, 'that barks at every bird he sees' (to quote Robert Burton on his own approach to writing): some sort of discrimination is clearly *de rigueur*. And his itinerary is never quite as random as he would have us believe.

My own sallies out into the world, if you'd like to know, are usually more like casual rendezvous than aimless strolls – I was, after all, at least christened a Presbyterian. All the same, these sallies are not study tours – I am generally uninterested in Truth – anything universal, really. My eye is caught by particularities. Truth I leave to God and Phillip Adams.

But it's hard for anyone in the modern world, I think, to wander haphazardly any more – and that's what idleness entails, even if the wandering is just in your mind. This is the age of ambulance-chasing, not ambling about. It's hard to take a break from self-consciousness, as historian Sarah Engledow, the curator of the National Portrait Gallery exhibition 'Idle Hours' put it, a break from performance, to quell restlessness and the longing for entertainment, to take pleasure in what she called 'unremarked moments'.

Unless you have a developed spiritual consciousness, it's difficult to allay the fear that, if you turn inwards to see what you might see, you will find nothing. Once upon a time there was at least the suspicion that you might find God lurking there or the Kingdom of Heaven.

Now, interestingly, most of the people in the paintings in the 'Idle Hours' exhibition – a collection of portraits of people who shaped Australia – were women – women or children. You'd think, given our new-found interest in what women have to say, that this would be a plus in the modern era. There was a man watering the garden, for instance, and another man reading the paper at a window, and another man lying on the floor listening to music, but the rest were mostly women – chatting, knitting, snoozing, drinking tea, or, like Bonnard's wife in so many of his paintings, just contentedly sitting. Do women, like children and dogs, have a special aptitude for enjoying idle hours, or have they simply had to adapt for social reasons over centuries – at least women of a certain class – to leading contented lives without being the slaves of 'industry'? Whatever the reason, it seems plausible to suggest that women are better at idleness (at leisured pensiveness, at stillness and taking pleasure in the ordinary) than men. Perhaps that's why you never see men engrossed in needlepoint.

But here's the paradox: traditionally, they write few essays. They're perfectly placed to write them (from my point of view), but do so far less often than men. The modern editor of an essays anthology will usually go out of his or her way to make sure that half the essays are by women – I strove for gender balance myself when editing *The Best Australian Essays* – but I can guarantee that any broad survey collection you pick up, even for recent decades, will draw overwhelmingly on male essayists. Some of you will see the patriarchy at work here, some of you other social factors, but for me it's a paradox I can't quite fathom. It's as if women have found other things to do with their time, things more to their liking than writing essays.

One commentator, Phillip Lopate, has suggested that it has something to do with what he calls the tone of gentlemanly authority, the sense of 'natural' authority, which the authors of the traditional essay have tended to enjoy, even when affecting self-doubt. This is a tone that, until very recently indeed (and even then it won't be 'gentlemanly'), fewer women than men are likely to have mastered. 'Ladylike authority' won't quite do, will it? It sounds too headmistressy, too prim, too performed.

I've been wondering if Lopate's suggestion could be phrased in another way. I've been wondering if women are as likely to want to address unknown friends as men are; if they might not be, in general, more comfortable addressing friends they know. Perhaps women do not dawdle in public, as the personal essayist does. Perhaps women indeed only *have* friends they know, so perhaps the whole idea of revealing yourself to 'unknown friends' seems odd to them. A woman intent on revealing herself, in other words, might more naturally turn to other genres – the short story, for instance, or the novel, the memoir, the autobiography – in which nakedness is more acceptable, like nudes in the Vatican Museum. Here nakedness is art. And make no mistake: the personal essay (unlike its more impersonal cousin) is a remarkably naked form. Your peculiarities, your frailties and quirks, your impotence in the face of life's vicissitudes, your predilections, your old wounds, your creaking bones are all not just there for all to see, but are your stock-in-trade.

In other words, yes, you must be adept at idleness, but you must also see it as your *right* – almost your birthright (playing on the notion of aristocracy) – if you want to be free to ramble through the world remarking at your leisure on the unremarked-upon. The essayist revels in a kind of ownership of the world. And this still has, I think, the whiff of gentlemanliness about it. But perhaps this will fade.

Meanwhile, as you'll have gathered, I can't help wondering if the essay – at least in its more personal form: the polemical essay is, I'm sure, quite safe – might be not quite of these times (a bit like singing 'God Save the Queen' or fondue dinners). The air of the aristocratic amateur that the essayist affects is out of favour. We don't approve of aristocrats and despise amateurs. I doubt, for instance, that Charles Lamb would find a publisher for his essays today, unless, as a friend of mine put it, he wrote a celebrity piece about his crazy sister stabbing their mother to death.

I'm selfishly concerned about the fate of the personal essay because it's what I most naturally do. I'm not a celebrity and well-researched trumpet blasts on the state of the world are not my strong point. I have rendezvous which ignite in me a desire to wheel around a target, affecting a nonchalant saunter, until I think I've nailed it. Irkutsk, the subjunctive, swearing, silence, Saturday afternoons – almost anything will do.

Well, anything that the voices in my head habitually talk about with passion.

Not cats, obviously, or Old Uzbek poetry.

So, have I nailed my target? I'm uncertain – but then uncertainty, except about matters of taste, is one of the flags that fly from the essayist's masthead. We're not averse to stabbing people in the back at times, but otherwise thrust is foreign to us – we circle, look over our shoulder, pause to greet passers-by, sniff the air and lurch a lot. For us the underlying air of incoherence that characterises our thought is something to be joyfully acknowledged – it's what makes us who we are. We don't want our dentist to be incoherent, but then we're not dentists.

And for us, at root – and let me quote Michel de Montaigne one last time – the greatest thing in the world is to know how to belong to oneself.

⁓

Much better, in fact, than knowing yourself. Not knowing ourselves, according to Pessoa – a contrary man, but acute – is a gift from the gods. Not knowing ourselves, he said, is a kind of lifeblood of the spirit. It keeps the soul from growing anaemic.

Idleness and ambling – bewitching time, in other words, instead of serving it – are vital to another art we are losing sight of, while talking about it almost obsessively: travel.

To be frank, I have talked about travel almost obsessively myself – over dinner, at seminars, at literary festivals and on the radio. I talk about it more than I do it. Travel itself, in my experience, mostly consists of eating and waiting and feeling anxious, but it is one of the few things in life that is worth doing for its own sake. At a certain age, when long-term goals seem pointless, this is immensely appealing. When I do get round to it, I tend to travel rather timidly. I feel uncomfortable, in all honesty, a bit of a fake, talking about it at all within earshot of real travellers, the ones who cross Borneo on foot, walk from Putney to Istanbul and so on, facing tarantulas and marauding natives, weeping with fatigue and putting themselves in mortal danger. Beside their Richard Burtons, I feel like some sort of Anita Brookner. The minotaurs that I face I tend to meet in cafés and hotel foyers. This is mildly depressing. But I can't help holding forth on the subject. And, when I do, this is the sort of thing I generally say.

At first glance travel might seem to be in its heyday: we've never left home for the airport in greater numbers. No weekend newspaper or magazine is complete without a glossy supplement on vacationing; every time you turn on the television some schoolchild has just scaled Mount Everest or a disabled octogenarian has kayaked backwards across the Tasman; even our cooking programs have turned into programs about travelling cooks, tossing things in woks in Kuala Lumpur or shopping for spices in Moroccan souks; and English eccentrics seem to be criss-crossing the globe with television crews these days in alarming numbers in search of . . . well, it's not quite clear what they're searching for (Stephen Fry visiting every state in the USA, for instance; David Heathcote reliving the Orient Express experience; Griff Rhys Jones and his dog boating up and down half the rivers in England). In short, everyone's on the move these days, but are they *travelling*?

For well over two millennia, men (and they almost all *were* men) boarded ships, climbed into wagons or simply walked out into the world to find out what was there. Men also left home to conquer, trade and loot a lot, as we know. But ever since Herodotus the Greek (the first recorded traveller in the modern sense of the word) they have also wandered the world in search of enlightenment, self-knowledge and paradise. Whatever pirates, soldiers, merchants and Christopher Columbus might have headed for the horizon in pursuit of, these are what *travellers* have set their sights on since the early Iron Age.

Almost within living memory, though, something has changed, at least for Westerners. Travelling to know the world today is pointless: in the space of a lifetime, the whole world has become known. In fact, I can see most of it, including a friend's new back shed in Hertfordshire, in minute detail on Google Earth. (I have just heard the author of an acclaimed book on North Korea talking on the radio: she has *only* visited North Korea through Google Earth.) Nobody needs to go on a pilgrimage to find themselves any more, either – a new self can be bought for a reasonable charge at a seminar, while bliss now comes in pills and bottles. Pilgrimage for Westerners has been laicised: we seek out places where we think certain cultural ideals might be enshrined – Lourdes, Uluru, the Guggenheim in Bilbao – but not to queue-jump into paradise.

No, instead of travelling to find the source of the Nile, which is now clearly marked on every map, or to worship at some saint's tomb, which makes it look as if you believe in salvation, or to amplify your sense of who you are, which is what the internet is for, men (and even some women) now travel to be the first to pogo-hop across Poland. They follow the Way of St James just for a lark, practically bungee-jumping into Santiago de Compostela, not even knowing who James was, let alone to expiate their sins. The easier it has become to leave home, the less reason there seems to be to do so.

Two thousand years ago or more, there were plenty of good reasons. Despite the dangers, Phoenicians, Greeks and Romans were amazingly adventurous travellers. Wealthy Romans, for example, not only hired holiday villas at beach resorts and wangled package deals at star-rated inns (often centrally heated with shopping arcades attached) as we might today, but they set off around the Mediterranean with guidebooks and maps in hand to visit architectural curiosities and shrines. They built a ring-road around the Mediterranean and cleared the highways of bandits and the seas of pirates, not *just* to make seeing the world easier (they also wanted to own it) – enlightenment, in some broad sense, was part of it. Incredible as it may sound, at about the time the Romans built the Colosseum, they actually reached Vietnam.

Empires are good for travel – Marco Polo only got to China, after all, thanks to the Pax Mongolica. So once the Roman Empire began to decline and fall, travel options also narrowed. In the medieval period, scholars and clerics moved about Europe between centres of learning, pilgrims went about their business of bargaining with paradise, and merchants kept on braving bandits and risking shipwreck to set up their trading networks as they had always done. But the world's most adventurous travellers until the Portuguese and Spaniards set out to conquer the earth were probably Muslim scholars and merchants, men such as Ibn Battuta, whose fourteenth-century voyages spanned the globe from West Africa to China. Muslims didn't have an empire as such, but they had the next best thing: the Dar al-Islam or House of Islam, which gave Moroccans a foothold in Sumatra, Omanis in East Africa and Egyptians in Guangzhou.

However, it was in Restoration England, surely, where medieval superstitions were giving way to a far more enlightened, scientific approach to knowledge, that travel turned into a national enterprise. In the age of Newton, Boyle and the flourishing Royal Society, the world was no longer simply 'God's handiwork', to be argued over by theologians: it was there to be illuminated by inquiring, rational minds. And put to good use as well, naturally.

Eventually, when the British Empire was at its height, when comfortable steamships began circling the globe and railway networks crossed continents, another kind of traveller emerged into the spotlight: the seeker after paradise. There was nothing new about the spiritual quest in itself: even in ancient Greece people risked life and limb to gather at sites of sacred significance in the hope of some kind of transforming experience. What was new about the kind of wandering undertaken by Freya Stark between the wars in the Middle East, or the Russian convert to Islam, Isabelle Eberhardt in North Africa a century ago, was the desire to find a place to belong to (not to own); a place where time would no longer press as it did in the regimented West, a spiritual homeland where rationalist, European notions of the self and of salvation would lose their power. Often this homeland was found in Islamic lands where certain Europeans – one thinks of Sir Richard Burton, T. E. Lawrence, Gertrude Bell and Wilfred Thesiger, for instance – found a level of authenticity in daily life in desert landscapes that had long since disappeared in Western Europe. For some people, unless they physically left Europe, it seemed impossible to find the right 'psychic observation post', as Carl Jung put it, from which to examine and understand their own psychological core.

When Freya Stark ventured out alone on a donkey, or even on foot, into the wildest parts of Persia, Yemen and Arabia, sleeping under the stars or in the homes of hospitable locals, she was looking for somewhere to be reborn. Like Burton and Lawrence, she wasn't above combining her journeys in the Orient with a bit of work in support of the Empire, but it would be a mistake to underestimate her genuine desire to reroot herself in a land where 'history' had an entirely different meaning. At some level, when we check in to our resort hotel in Bali or Barbados, we too are seeking rebirth, it seems to me: in the pristine hotel room with its starched sheets and sea views, in the period of timelessness and absence of toil, we too seek a banal kind of blessedness, nurturing the hope that our spirit will be cleansed. 'Unspoiled Thailand', the brochure promises, or 'the real Borneo', as if a quickie getaway tour were all it took to re-enter the Garden of Eden and start our lives all over again (avoiding apples this time).

Paradise isn't really paradise, though, unless you can reinvent yourself sexually. The whole point about paradise is that it was where the idea of sex originated. No work, plenty of free food and sex – that was paradise. If the brochures are to be believed, a lot of people think it still is. The men's toilets at airports aren't furnished with condom machines for nothing: making whoopee is what 'going to a place where I can be more fully myself' often means. And before we throw up our hands in horror and start muttering darkly about sex tourists in Bangkok, we'd do well to remind ourselves that sexual self-discovery always has been a strong motive for travel, whether in the guise of husband-hunting, befriending the locals or openly revolting against the moral code in force at home. Once the Grand Tour became popular for upper-class Englishmen in the mid-seventeenth century, there was no disguising one of travel's main attractions – and it wasn't just exploring the roots of Western civilisation.

In fact, there is hardly a famous traveller you can mention from any age who was not attracted by the possibility of sexual adventure while penetrating the unknown.

Freya Stark in her Middle Eastern travels was looking for something else as well, something that was comparatively new: beauty. For most of human history, travellers had been barely aware of what millions today travel exclusively to enjoy: beautiful vistas, beautiful landscapes. When Freya Stark contemplated, with rapture, a desert sunset or dawn in a mountain wilderness, or when she consciously savoured the magical blending of colours, sounds and fragrances in some faraway city, believing that this moment alone was justification enough for being there, she was doing what comparatively few humans before her had done.

When Herodotus went to Egypt or Babylon, for example, in the fifth century BC, it never occurred to him to use the word 'beautiful' to describe a scene – he reserved it for the human form. A scene might please the eye because of its promise of refreshment or fertility, or its historical significance, but not until the Romantic period in the late eighteenth century did Europeans commonly seek out views and landscapes in order simply to enjoy their beauty. Nowadays we do it incessantly, but do we know why? Why must our hotel room have a 'beautiful view'? Because, as moderns, we still want paradise, but we want it right here, now, and a picture postcard view is about as close as we can expect to come to it.

Now that the world is more or less known and leisure travel has replaced the quest for peace with God, great travellers in the historical sense are few on the ground. We travel differently now if we leave home at all, and, not sure about why we're putting ourselves to all this trouble, we use different words to describe our motivations: 'recreation', 'leisure', 'adventure' and 'business', all of them parodic versions of what once was possible. The idler's moment has arrived.

The skilled idler now has a chance to exploit a core reason for travelling that has survived, at least in our subconscious: sometimes we still leave home and wander about the world to magnify our idea of who we are as human beings by looking at ourselves in a much vaster mirror of humanity than is possible at home. In Tunis or La Paz we will ask ourselves questions about what it feels like to be someone completely different from ourselves – questions we're less likely to ask in Brisbane, say. We travel to be transported. It might not make us wiser, but leaving home, we hope, hazily, might make us feel more intensely alive.

But will it?

Not everyone has thought so. 'Only extreme feebleness of imagination can justify anyone needing to travel in order to feel,' says Pessoa in his *Book of Disquiet*. But this is nonsense, surely. Would he have said the same thing about reading? Or loving? Has 'someone who has sailed every sea' *really* 'merely sailed the monotony of himself', as this Portuguese curmudgeon claimed? It may well be a twentieth-century classic, this *Book of Disquiet* (which I dip into when I'm feeling autumnal), and almost lethally elegant – the drop from poetic high-mindedness to the banality of the poet's own cramped life leaves you sick at heart – but he's a curmudgeon, nonetheless, not a *bel esprit*, as Montaigne was. Life is just a bow that comes undone, he says. Very clever, deftly modernist, a striking metaphor, but that's not really how anyone I know feels about it. Or was I indeed simply trying to reknot the bow of my life when I agreed to go to Vladivostok?

A few years ago I had one of my rendezvous in Vladivostok and pottered over to Irkutsk in southern Siberia while I was in the neighbourhood, as it were. When I got back I reported in *The Monthly* on what I had experienced.

Vladivostok

The first thing I did in my Vladivostok hotel room while waiting for hot water to reach the seventh floor (which it never did, not in five days, although I understand they were wallowing in hot baths twice a day on the fourth) was to turn on the television. Just a few minutes of commercials, soapies and the latest news in some exotic tongue, I generally find, and you know you're somewhere thrillingly foreign.

Actually, you know you're somewhere foreign, if not quite thrillingly, from the moment you board your Vladivostok Air flight in Seoul, despite the flat Australian voice telling you what to do, if you can be bothered, in the event of an emergency. For many foreigners, taking a Babyflot flight, as they're called in the post-Soviet era, of any kind is emergency enough in itself.

The image that first flashed onto the television screen that evening was of Peter Cundall, the lovable talking garden gnome from *Gardening Australia*, throwing blood and bone about and enthusing as only he can about broad beans. I was aghast. CNN in Vladivostok is one thing – one expects CNN to appear on television screens in hotel rooms wherever one is, except possibly in Pyongyang – but Peter Cundall was another matter entirely. I did not want to be whisked back to Tasmania the moment I arrived in Vladivostok.

After all, Vladivostok had been part of my dreaming, as it were, a key strand in my psychological make-up, since early childhood. The snaps my father showed me of Vladivostok, taken, I imagine, in about 1918, are the first photographs I can remember looking at. Small, square, yellowing photographs curling at the edges . . . Hills, old houses, ships at anchor . . . Try as I might, I can't remember much more. But they planted a seed – indeed, several seeds – in my lush, childish mind. Over the years they burgeoned into the conviction that I must leave home and see the world like my father – and not just the places comfortably-off aunts sent us postcards from, not just London or Rome or, on some madly adventurous fling, Cairo and the Pyramids, but forbidden places as well, such as Vladivostok. (And Vladivostok, being a naval base, was forbidden territory until only a decade ago – officially, that is, 'forbidden' being the actual Russian word that was used.) And those yellowing photographs – at least, I think they were yellowing, but then at my age everything from one's childhood is slightly sepia-tinted – also implanted in me the desire to go to Russia. Irrationally, even foolishly, but it did.

And I went, many times, but never to Siberia or the Far East. And now there I was. The Bolshevik Revolution that had reached the Pacific a few years after my father had sailed into Vladivostok's Golden Horn inlet (not quite Istanbul, but you can see the resemblance) was just a stirring memory, reduced to a cluster of exhibits in the local museum; my father the merchant seaman was an increasingly fuzzy memory; and the little boy who had dreamt zigzaggingly of being adventurous was now a rather sedate middle-aged man. But there I was. In Vladivostok.

Nowadays, I thought to myself, reaching over to switch off Peter Cundall, everywhere is just anywhere. Even Vladivostok. It takes a tremendous effort of the will now, it takes imagination and a ferreting knowledge of history to turn what the eye sees into a richly layered, living city, to understand (and perhaps love) what the city surrounding you alludes to. Would I be up to the task?

The phone rang – goodness me, they were quick off the mark – and a silky female voice, in elegant, almost nineteenth-century Russian, inquired as to whether I was desirous of spending time with some young ladies that evening. In the plural. I'm not sure how she ever managed to drum up any business at the Hotel Vladivostok over the telephone – there were garishly dressed young ladies trawling up and down the corridor outside my door all night. 'Batting for the other team' was not an expression my caller seemed familiar with, however, so she tried again the next night, and the next night, and the night after that.

⁓

In fact, Vladivostok wasn't just anywhere, I discovered. It's not the Russian San Francisco, as Nikita Khrushchev declared it would be, although it's magnificently sited on a hilly peninsula between two vast bays dotted with forested islands, and has trams. It's itself – a slightly down-at-heel, provincial port at the end of the Trans-Siberian Railway, nine hours flying time from Moscow. And, although its hills are these days covered in the usual post-Bauhaus nightmare of grim-faced apartment blocks, the centre of town, down beside the Golden Horn near the station, has a kind of smile on its face. It may have been painted on a little crookedly – one should not peer too closely, perhaps – but on a sunny morning in early autumn it had a certain charm.

The old buildings (well, not so very old: the peninsula was first settled by Russians in 1860) – the banks, hotels, office buildings and apartment blocks, now being carefully restored, as well as the magnificent terminus of the Trans-Siberian Railway – are elegant examples of nineteenth-century neoclassicism with some modernist touches. Cream, dove blue, pale green, apricot, white. Strolling along the tree-lined streets past all the new cafés, upmarket clothing shops and, of course, computer outlets, I could almost have been (except for the computers) in some Mediterranean port city still waiting for its ship to come in . . . half a century ago.

It's not the architecture or lack of modern appurtenances that make me say 'half a century ago', it's the mysterious sparseness (I can think of no other word) of the downtown area of many Russian provincial cities, and Vladivostok is no exception. It doesn't feel like a city over half the size of Brisbane. It feels more like Townsville. It does, however, have that slightly frisky edge that port cities have all over the world.

Its reputation is less for friskiness, though, than for outright corruption, violence and skullduggery on an unequalled scale in post-Soviet Russia – which is saying something. Is this why in the main bookshop in the town centre the biggest section is Crime? A bit of sheng fui, a cookery book or two, a couple of shelves of American pulp fiction – and then acres of Crime. 'Don't walk around the city at night,' I was told more than once. 'You see nobody out there on the street?' my driver asked as we drove from the airport into town the first night. 'That's because they know better. Take a bus, take a taxi – don't walk.'

I walked. Very late on the Sunday night I walked through the middle of the city with a couple of women friends and was attacked by no one more alarming than a gaggle of Scientologists handing out pamphlets. It's Dianetics now, apparently, not dialectical materialism. Still, to be fair, three slightly dowdy diners well past their prime were always unlikely to be a target for international smuggling rings. Serious muggers were probably loitering outside the many casinos and nightclubs. In any case, we'd just had dinner in an underground restaurant set up in an old NKVD torture chamber – violence and skullduggery were nothing new in the Wild East.

⁓

The midnight Scientologists were no surprise. The New Age is coming into luxuriant flower all over Russia, I'm told. After all, for decades Russians were forced to stick to the highways of scientific rationalism, and it was a pretty grim march, so people are understandably curious nowadays about all the intriguing byways of human thinking that were for so long closed off to them. There's even a new curiosity about the old animist beliefs and rituals of the peoples who once lived beyond the Urals – and still do, although in dwindling numbers. As dotty as Dianetics, some might say, but shamanism is unquestionably venerable. Its echoes can still be heard in so-called 'farmers' music' (*samul-nori*) in nearby Korea and the Japanese are practising it to this day, with spellbinding panache, in their Shinto shrines just across the water.

Not much else, though, from the millennia before the Russians arrived seems to have survived. In the museums – and Russians love their museums, they love tidy tableaux of how it once was (a paleolithic campsite, a Tungus house, a governor's ball) – there are sometimes small displays of hunters hunting, say, or a tribal housewife, elaborately costumed, sitting rather vacantly in her tribal kitchen. But everyone I met seemed pretty vague about who and what was here before the Russians arrived. Just tribes. In point of fact, near relatives of the tribal housewife in the museum invaded China in the seventeenth century and ruled it as the Manchu dynasty for three hundred years.

Russians, like Australians in their own country until recently, still seem strangely comfortable with the idea of taking over native lands – Siberia and the Far Eastern territories in their case. They have a word, which appears as bold as brass on museum labels everywhere I went, to describe the process we might now call 'invasion'. It's *osvoyenie* and it means simply to make something your own, to master it – it might be a new DVD player or it might be Siberia. In fact, my Russian–English dictionary merrily translates *osvoyenie krainego severa* as 'the opening up of the far north'. Who could object to a bit of opening up? The Cossacks, generals, explorers and traders who opened up this part of the world are still unequivocally heroes. That's the trouble with the Chechens, you see, as a friend explained to me beside the memorial to those who had died in the war in Chechnya (Russians, not Chechens). Give them back their country and you never know where it will end. Next thing you know, the Buryats, Yakuts and God knows who else will want their lands back as well.

On my last day in Vladivostok I visited a little museum devoted to the life of a celebrated Far Eastern explorer, Vladimir Arsenyev. I looked at photographs of V. K. Arsenyev, letters he'd written, the table he'd written them on, his typewriter, his gramophone, the tent he'd slept in on his expeditions around the Far East – the usual collection of odds and ends you get in museums set up in the houses of famous people. Quite often he'd travel with a native companion, so I asked the guide if he spoke any of the local languages. 'Oh, yes,' she said, without a trace of embarrassment, 'he spoke all of them. They're so primitive, you see – no problem at all for someone as brilliant as Arsenyev to master.'

⁓

'Tasmania – yes, I've been there.' My new friend was a slightly inebriated middle-aged man called Igor, who had insisted I join him and his pal Boris at their table in the Cosy Cabin Bar on the fourth floor (the one with plenty of hot water). 'I'm an ethnologist,' he went on, 'so I've seen all those pygmies and crocodiles of yours in Tasmania – very interesting.' It was already a very Russian sort of conversation.

By this time I was feeling a little light-headed from the smell of Russian food – not queasy but light-headed. After all, wafting in and out of all my memories of Russia in my student days in Moscow, when we were constantly craving to be fed, is the smell of food. Or at least the dizzying promise of food in the gusts of warm air that enveloped you when you stepped into a restaurant, café or cafeteria.

Nobody ever went to Russia to sample the classy cuisine – at least, not in my day, not in the 1960s and 1970s. You might have gone for the ballet, the paintings or the palaces, or because *War and Peace* (or perhaps *Das Kapital*) was your favourite work of fiction, but nobody to my knowledge ever went there for the food. There is, after all, only so much you can do with pig's foot brawn, lukewarm cabbage pies and meatballs with boiled buckwheat. It's all quite filling and tasty if you're famished, with an appealing whiff of Tartary to it, but, like Bulgarian throat-singing, a little of this sort of peasanty fare goes a remarkably long way.

The misty-eyed émigrés I knew before I first went to Russia were wont to conjure up a lost world of steaming samovars, storerooms full of pickled gherkins and homemade jams, and frozen barrels of sauerkraut out in the snow. In Moscow in the mid-1960s, there were indeed gherkins, jam and sauerkraut to be had, but (at least in the student cafeteria in winter) not much else. I remember whole meals of mashed potato swimming in gravy and sprinkled with dill, with a glass of strongly sugared black tea to follow. There were restaurants for foreigners and the Soviet elite, naturally, where the kinds of dishes you find in Russian cookery books (fish soups, *borshch*, crumbed chicken fillets, pilaf and so on) were on the menu, if not always actually on offer, but getting into one was such a Byzantine rigmarole of bluster and string-pulling that few of us students ever made it.

As a result we were ravenous all the time. We lived in an unending haze of desire for food. We plotted all day how, where and what to eat. A night at the Bolshoi was an exciting prospect, but even more thrilling was the thought of the smoked salmon on thickly buttered bread or the bowls of ice-cream with a dollop of stewed fruit on sale during the two intervals. A visit to a friend's flat was an emotional and intellectual adventure, but the herrings! The anchovies on eggs! The tinned crab in mayonnaise! An expedition to see some ancient, amazingly frescoed church outside Moscow may have been an unforgettable experience, but the highlight of the day was lunch in a hotel restaurant – beetroot and frankfurter soup, with dollops of sour cream; schnitzel, fried potatoes and slices of pickled cucumber; pancakes and cream cheese . . . The mere memory of the joy of a lunch like this – hideously expensive, served with a studied surliness, coffee like dishwater, but who cared? – is enough to make me weep with nostalgia.

Curiously enough, one thing we were practically rolling in was caviar. Ideally, of course, it should be served cold in a chilled crystal dish, then spread delicately on buttered toast or bliny, but we ate it spread thickly like jam on chunks of white bread. We also ate it straight – just forked out of tins into our eager mouths (black or red, there was plenty of both). It's a luxury again nowadays, of course, since the sturgeon have been killed off. In the almost unbearably chichi Stockman supermarket in Moscow, I noticed recently that the pale-grey kind sells for about $1000 a kilo.

In the new Russia, even in some provincial towns, you can now find, at least in the better class of restaurant, all the refinements of international cuisine, even truffle shavings in your soup, if that's what you're really looking for. After all, they've been globalised. Not, however, in the Cosy Cabin Bar of my hotel in Vladivostok. There I was reduced to *pel'meni* – a sort of Russian version of wonton soup.

'What do you do?' said my new ethnographer friend, eyeing me with that hint of resentment mixed with cat-and-mouse playfulness you get a lot of in Russia.

'I'm a writer.'

'Do you have any *great* writers in Australia?'

'Well,' I said, 'without wanting to get too postmodern about what "great" means, yes, we have . . . well, we had Patrick White, for instance.' I'd thought of mentioning David Malouf or Helen Garner, but decided against it, under the circumstances.

'Never heard of him,' Igor said, quaffing an alarming amount of vodka from his glass in one gulp. 'Have you, Borya?' Boris hadn't heard of White either. 'You see, the trouble with your country is that there are no *great* Australians. Can you name any *great* Australians?'

Donald Bradman clearly wouldn't do. Nor would Kylie Minogue. 'Well . . .' I began, hoping a suitable name would pop into my head, but strangely enough my mind was a blank. Surely *someone* in our history had been great.

'In Russia, on the other hand, we have lots of great writers, great poets, great scientists and great ethnographers. My grandfather was a prince, by the way. Do you have princes?'

'No,' I said, 'not as such.' Should I mention Our Mary in Copenhagen?

'This used to be a great country,' Igor went on, with Boris nodding sagely on the sidelines. 'A very great country. A mighty country. And now it's all in ruins. Now I have to get a visa to visit my own brother in Kiev.'

At this point he fell sound asleep and slumped sideways at a dangerous angle in his chair. Boris pulled him upright, murmuring tenderly in his ear.

'The most powerful nation on earth,' Igor said suddenly, returning in a burst of lucidity directly to the fray. 'You can't say that about Australia.'

'No, you can't,' I agreed. 'But do you think you're happier now than before . . . ?'

'The collapse? No. What is there to feel happier about? We are no longer powerful and I have to get a visa to visit my own brother in Kiev.'

I was about to mention the now abundant supply of good food, the fashionable clothes available in every second store, the mobile phones, affordable Japanese cars (the traffic jams here are worse than in Rome), the trips to Japan and Korea (and theoretically to

Tasmania), when Igor's attention switched abruptly to the honey-coloured cleavage of the waitress bending over him with the bill. I murmured something apologetic and made a break for it.

'Mister!' he called out as I headed out the door. 'Give me your email address. I want to stay in touch.'

Hastily scrawling pygmy@utas.edu.au on a damp napkin, I made for the lift.

∽

Like the waitress with honey-coloured breasts, all the young women on the streets of Vladivostok are beautiful. It strikes you immediately. They all have shining hair and flawless complexions, they are all svelte, they are all dressed to kill. The Americans at the conference I was attending couldn't believe their eyes. Where are all the dumpy ones, they kept asking, the sea-cows in XXXL t-shirts? Where indeed were the merely plain? The young men, too – and almost everyone on the streets of Vladivostok is young – seemed to have stepped from the pages not so much of *GQ* as some sports magazine with a slight homoerotic whiff to it: shaven-headed, angular, wasp-waisted, perfect, like hard-hearted angels. They were almost bow-legged with virility.

And where, for that matter, were the crones and sour-smelling old men in grubby overcoats of Soviet times? At home in the suburbs, mouldering away in those vast estates of high-rise flats? They certainly weren't visible on the streets. I only ventured into the suburbs once, catching a bus to a shopping mall, but they weren't there either. The mall looked like Fountain Gate.

Everyone in Vladivostok, without exception, was talking on a mobile phone. Even in Korea only half the population is talking on a mobile at any given moment, while here everybody had one clamped to his or her ear all the time. According to the statistics, and judging by the state of the streets, gridlocked with traffic at peak hour, half the population also now has a car. (Japanese, of course. To drive a Russian car is to risk jeers and catcalls from other motorists.) The new status symbol, on sale, it seemed, in every second shop, is the laptop. Computers – well, who doesn't have a computer? Yes, a new laptop might cost you half a year's salary, if you're a teacher or civil servant on $4000 a year, but anyone who's anyone must have one. In terms of consumer technology, at least, Vladivostok could be . . . well, anywhere.

∽

'Veneer' is the word that comes to mind when I think about what I saw in Russia. I don't say it with a sneer – it's perfectly understandable.

This word seemed particularly appropriate in Irkutsk, three thousand kilometres to the north-west of Vladivostok, close to the Mongolian border. (Too close, some would hint darkly – all over town the abandoned factories and half-finished buildings were swarming, it seemed, with illegal immigrants from China, Vietnam and Mongolia, engaged for the most part in nefarious activities better left unspecified.)

From its beginnings as a wooden fortress on the Angara River in the mid-seventeenth century, Irkutsk grew into an opulent hub of empire. It was in the handsome mansions and government offices of Irkutsk, not in distant St Petersburg, that the *osvoyenie* of the Pacific territories, and ultimately Alaska – even the colonisation of California – was planned; it was in the lavish churches of Irkutsk (where once again the iconostases are gleaming, the candles are burning and plaintive women's voices soar in song) that prayers for the success of these missions were offered; from Irkutsk that settlers spread out across the taiga to hunt, mine, trade and plough the land. In some ways Irkutsk became Russia's Mexico City or Lima: the capital of the motherland's far-flung dominions. The city's coat-of-arms showed a running tiger with a sable in its mouth – 'bloodthirsty, strong and ferocious', as one chronicler proudly described it.

The veneer of modernity bamboozles the senses, though, blinding you to both the real Irkutsk of today and the dream-city underpinning it. To be honest, wandering its streets and squares today – only in the daylight, just to be on the safe side – I could barely make out the phantom Irkutsk underlying the city of today at all'. In the centre of the city, for instance, on the banks of the Angara, as you stroll along Karl Marx or Lenin Streets (there's even still a Dzerzhinsky Street, named after the head of the secret police), the lethal traffic, the displays of plasma TV sets and Armani's latest couture, the advertisements for holidays in Thailand and the political activists pamphleteering on street corners dull the resonances we might have hoped to pick up of the old 'capital' of the new territories. The neoclassical and Siberian baroque buildings – even a handful of churches – are still there, but are strangely mute. Avenues that might easily have blossomed into a rue de la Paix or boulevard des Italiens (in a soft light – well, it did call itself the Paris of Siberia) are merely cacophonous bazaars. The dream-city has become commonplace.

And in behind the elegant old banks and townhouses of the rich, before you get to the serried ranks of Soviet-era apartment blocks, there is another, unvarnished, Irkutsk: street after street of sunken, wooden houses, without running water or sewerage, inhabited, I presume, by those too old to be bothered moving or too poor to pay the astronomical post-Soviet rents. They're oddly picturesque, in a gloomy, Siberian sort of way, especially the ones with lace-like fretted woodwork around the windows. You can imagine gaunt political exiles, freed from labour in the mines, huddling around the stove in one of these lopsided houses a century and a half ago, eating watery soup. Europe in those days was two months away by post-chaise. It still feels a long way away.

Your better class of exile, such as the Decembrist Prince Volkonsky, could call on wealthy relatives back in St Petersburg to build them something more befitting their station, naturally, and did. Indeed, his elegant wooden mansion on a backstreet near the river (which I finally got into after an altercation with a gang of urchins) became a glittering cultural hub in Irkutsk in the middle of the nineteenth century: soirées, masked balls, banquets, theatrical performances, concerts by visiting artists from France and Germany, all easily imagined as you stroll through the spacious, exquisitely furnished rooms – alone, in my case, as I always was in Irkutsk's museums. Attendants followed me around turning out the lights as I passed from room to room. It was disconcerting.

～

An hour's spectacular drive away through red and gold forests of birch and larch, I sat by Lake Baikal reading a salacious French novel, lifting my eyes occasionally to contemplate the astonishing snow-capped mountains on the opposite shore as well as what I had seen in Vladivostok and Irkutsk.

It was neither summer, the season for boating and swimming, nor winter, when skiers arrive from all over Russia and even beyond, so I was almost alone in the modern hotel above the lake. I was alone in the vast dining room, which smelt strongly of fish and ice-cream, alone on my walks along the lake, and almost alone in the museum by the lake shore, where I inspected stuffed seals, wolves and wolverines as well as bizarre creatures from the lake swimming in glass tanks. Company was possible, but I left the note in my room suggesting I ring a certain number 'to talk about having fun' for someone more adventurous to follow up on.

Coming down in the lift on the last morning in Vladivostok, the only other passenger, a young man with the regulation shaven skull, suddenly startled me by asking, 'What are you so sad about?'

I didn't actually feel sad. A little melancholy, perhaps, or wistful, but not sad. I did feel that something about Russia I'd once loved, something remarkable, was fading away, like a muffled melody, drowned out by the familiar, the international everyday. It's what we all wanted, of course, in the old days, all hoped for: Russia plus democracy and technology and shops with full shelves. But now it's here, we don't *love* it any more. Eros has fled. It's tempting to see it as a shabby version of home. Somewhere has become anywhere.

It hasn't really – I know that – and it never will. It is still a country where a stranger in a lift can suddenly say to you, 'What are you so sad about?', flinging you into a whirlpool of memories and half-remembered stories – tsars, battles, poems, novels, icons, cupolas, loves, madnesses – and endlessly spiralling conversations. One day I'll make my way back there to unearth this phantom city, still lying – I know it does – beneath the commonplace.

I haven't been back, though. In a funny sort of way I feel in my mid-sixties that I've put Russia to bed. Perhaps the lessons she had to teach me about who I might be have now been learnt or seem hopelessly quixotic. For the most part I am content just to stay at home, writing. Writers should be 'unhoused', as I think John Banville once said, but that's only possible if your sense of 'home' is deeply rooted. Can there be a more important word than 'home' to make your own in the English language? 'Love', I suppose, although I wonder sometimes if they might amount to much the same thing.

If I *were* to go somewhere, though, it would probably be somewhere in that sultry arc that stretches from Portugal eastwards to about India and then peters out. I can't fully explain what draws me to this particular swathe of lands and tongues and bodies, but there's something there that I can't find in Siberia or even Brazil. This is where I'd like to be footloose. I'd be happy to go anywhere on the planet with a purpose, even Belgium, but along that curve from Lisbon to Calcutta I feel a hunger to be footloose, to be unhoused while at the same time feeling curiously at home.

Richard Burton, the great Victorian traveller, and expert in everything Muhammadan, would have snorted and said the reason was obvious. In an essay at the end of his *Book of the Thousand Nights and a Night*, he purported to believe in the existence of something he called the Sotadic zone, named after the Greek poet Sotades, famous for his lewd satiric verses and sexual enthusiasms of a typically Mediterranean, third-century-BC kind. Burton, as far as I can work out, seems to have included most of the planet in his 'zone', apart from Africa south of the Arabs, northern Europe and Siberia, as well (it goes without saying) as Australia. In this zone, Burton assured his readers, 'the Vice' was both 'popular' and 'endemic', although he acknowledged that in 'great cities' everywhere modesty was apt to decay and pederasty to flourish. Berlin, for instance, he said, 'despite her strong flavour of Phariseeism, Puritanism and Chauvinism in religion, manners and morals, is not a whit better than her neighbours'. A city with a certain allure, in other words, but well north of his (and my) Sotadic zone.

I know what Burton was getting at, yet while my Sotadic zone is still an erotic one – that is to say, gnawed at by a kind of hunger for experience and simmering with possibilities of being masculine barely dreamt of in East Bentleigh or Brewarrina – its appeal for me at this point in my life has its source in something much deeper than eros: roots, the roots of my civilised self.

A glance at the atlas throws some light on the nature of my 'zone': it has something to do with the Silk Road, that network of trade routes stretching, since Alexander the Great pushed into Asia nearly two and a half millennia ago, from the Mediterranean across to India, China, even Java. The erotic pull weakens east of India, it's true, but my mind still likes to scurry along those arteries of culture and ideas (it wasn't solely about silk and spices, after all – far from it) from Cadiz all the way to Shanghai and back. Being so disconnected, I love the connectedness, I marvel at the transformations along the way (those wild rhubarb stalks in Tangut province in China ending up as a purgative in a porcelain dish at Whitehall). I love the notion of *crossroads*, the thought of Sogdians striking deals with Greeks, Nestorians arguing with Buddhists, Arabs setting up shop in Sumatra. So many of my childhood enthusiasms took flight from points along the Silk Road, too: from Tibet to all those Central Asian khanates, from Arab souks to silkworms – perhaps the idea of travel itself. Even Myoe's moon-mindedness once drifted along the Silk Road from India across China to Japan. When the trails grow faint (in Africa, say) or fade away altogether (in the Americas), my curiosity grows dull, my interest becomes merely polite.

For me the web is at its densest, its liveliest, its most evocative in Syria on the eastern edge of the Mediterranean. ('The Mediterranean is the human norm,' Cyril Fielding says with relief in *A Passage to India*, having just reached Venice after years in India. When you leave it, you 'approach the monstrous and extraordinary'.) Stand on the Grand Colonnade in Palmyra, for instance, in the desert between Damascus and the Euphrates, surrounded by the ruins – the *Greek* ruins – of the marketplace, the shops, the tombs, the caravanserais and vast temples to forgotten gods, all golden in the harsh sunlight, and you can feel that this was once a pulsing ganglion of Silk Roads. (Especially if you are there alone.) This is where Asia once met Greece and then Rome. Like Chang'an, Kashgar and Baghdad, Palmyra was a hub, with spokes radiating in every direction across the planet. We all spring from Palmyra.

Astonishingly, these days you can leave Tasmania late in the evening and be in Syria early the next morning. A bit of a snooze, breakfast and you're there. Once I knew this, the temptation to go became irresistible. For a couple of years I shilly-shallied, wondering how safe it would be, how welcoming, how truly different from anywhere else with mosques and ruins, and then all of a sudden I upped and went. Sometimes you just need a dose of enchantment.

Three weeks later, on the point of coming home, I wrote the following.

Postcard from Damascus

When I first stepped outside the walls of the Old City this morning, the sheer ugliness of Damascus nearly knocked me off my feet. Raucous, traffic-choked, yellowish squalor as far as the eye could see – it was like tumbling into the pit of Gehenna. In some ways it was a quintessentially Syrian experience.

For days I've just been mooching around the Old City in a dream, cocooned within its walls, time-travelling through the maze of its gloomy laneways, in and out of ancient mosques and palaces and churches. After all, that's why you come to Damascus: to time-travel. Well, it's supposed to be the oldest city in the world, although Jericho might give it a run for its money. Between the souk Midhat Pasha and the Thomas Gate you can soar up and down across millennia, swooping in and out of whole civilisations – three or four before lunch, if you feel like it: Arameans, Greeks, Romans, Mamelukes, Ottomans – take your pick. Now, suddenly, without any warning, I'd been catapulted back into the twenty-first century. I tried in vain to cross the road, stumbled over a dwarf selling cigarettes and beat a hasty retreat back into the Middle Ages.

It had happened so abruptly. One moment I was strolling through the arcaded souk amongst swarms of pilgrims heading for the mosque, dazzled by the seemingly infinite array of perfumes, silks, spices, ceramics, soaps, brasses, gold and silver – were the caravans perhaps still plying the Silk Road to Samarkand and China? – and the next moment I was outside, choking in the noxious fug of the New City. Pedestrians darted amongst the honking cars like startled rabbits – God help you if you were on a Zimmer frame or blind. Ramshackle buildings stretched away into the distance on every side. And everywhere I looked the oddly weak-chinned president was smiling down on the morass, sometimes in sunglasses (he's an ophthalmologist by training), always with the dictator's faint distaste for what he sees. In three weeks I have never heard a syllable whispered against him. At elections he gets about 98 per cent of the vote. An atheist I met in Aleppo railed for hours against the medieval ignorance Syria is sunk in, the suffocating obsession with religion, the misery of the people and men's ownership of women's bodies, but he never breathed a word of complaint about the Leader.

Until I came face to face with modern Damascus this morning, I felt very taken with it. More than that: the Old City enchanted me as neither Tunis nor Algiers had. Time evaporates here. I have sat, for instance, with a banana milkshake beside the Roman gate on the street called Straight – Saul must have ridden through it, blinded by his revelation on the road from Jerusalem – and been to the house of Ananias (now a tiny subterranean chapel), who laid his hands on Saul's eyes, restoring his sight, renaming him Paul and changing the course of history. There's almost no one about, oddly enough, except, of course, in the souk and the great Umayyad Mosque, but it's so vast that a thousand worshippers in its prayer halls and shimmering courtyard would still leave it feeling half empty. And to think that the Arameans were bowing down to their god Hadad in a temple on this spot three thousand years ago, and after them the Romans to Jupiter and then the Christians to their new-fangled triune deity in a massive basilica . . . And now here I am, drinking tea beneath its walls as the afternoon call to prayer rolls out from the minaret above me across the city. To no obvious effect, by the way, despite the ever-presence of religion. The shopkeepers keep dozing in the sun, the tourists keep ambling by wide-eyed, while the locals suck on their sheeshas (or hubbly-bubblies) without pause and chat with their friends, ending each sentence with *insh'Allah* ('God willing').

I wake up with a start in the dark every morning when the dawn call to prayer splits the air, but (according to the desk clerk at the hotel) nobody else does. He's a Muslim, he says, but the Five Pillars of Islam don't seem to figure largely in his daily life. In fact, I wonder if he could recite them off the top of his head. In Syria the air is thick with religion – you're Sunni, Druze, Alawite, Armenian Christian, Greek Orthodox, *something*, everyone is *something*. Just try saying you're a non-believer . . . Sometimes I found myself choking on religion, gasping for fresh air, but it wasn't like religion in the West: in Syria it's about what is right, it seemed to me, rather than what is true, it's about tradition and authority. 'Allah doesn't approve of keeping dogs in your house,' I was told – and, indeed, you only see dogs in the Christian quarter. (I stopped mentioning my dog after a day or two in Syria – the very idea of loving a dog seemed to cause a faint tremor of disgust.) There was no point in asking what the evidence was for this. Loving a dog was just wrong. It said so in the Quran. I was told this gently, as you might explain good manners to a child.

Yet I found an enchantment in the almost dogless Old City. I especially love those old Damascene houses like miniature mosques, opening out as you come through the half-hidden door from the street into a marble courtyard with the rooms in galleries high above it. My hotel here is like that. I sit there by the fountain for hours at a time sipping tea and thinking, just thinking about everything, just letting my imagination take flight. It's hard to do that at home.

In a sense, Syria itself has been like this: it's not a beautiful country, it's harsh and rocky and a tawny-yellow, almost treeless, with no wild animals ('We've killed them all') and littered with ugly tawny-yellow towns. Yet dotted about this brutal landscape are small havens of extraordinary beauty where, if you choose your moment well, you can be virtually alone, outside time, stripped of everything you are at home. You're unlikely to be alone in Krak des Chevaliers, the crusader citadel near the coast, which is packed with mobs of Germans and Italians from sunrise to dusk. Or in the souk in Aleppo, of course, unless you go there very early in the morning, which would be rather pointless since its magic can work on you only when the shutters come down and its treasures cascade into its aromatic alleyways. And even here you have secrets within secrets – silent shrines and empty courtyards glimpsed through doorways as you pass.

But elsewhere you really can find yourself alone in some marvel from hundreds, even thousands, of years ago. Out in the desert towards Iraq, for example, I came across a huge abandoned citadel from the eighth century, the East Wall Palace, which once guarded the route into Mesopotamia, just standing there, empty for the last seven hundred years, its towers and walls intact, and I wandered through it alone. At one point I wondered if I was hallucinating the whole thing. Even in Palmyra, where hordes of tourists arrive each day in buses from Damascus, the ruins are so vast – the temples and colonnaded streets, the theatre, agora, baths, ovens and ruined houses – that even here, if you choose your moment, you can sit alone in complete silence on some fallen column, contemplating the magnificence of this Silk Road metropolis, in decline since Aurelius put it to the torch 1700 years ago. It's unearthly, this soundless, toppling splendour in a wilderness of sand and stone.

Take the mountaintop monastery of Mar Musa near the Lebanese border, founded in the sixth century by the son of the king of Abyssinia. It's in every guidebook I've seen, but it's a long climb on foot to where it's perched, so when you get there, it's empty, even at the height of the season. There's a monk or two gliding about, and a few cooing doves, but basically you're on your own here, free to pretend that it's still the sixth century – to pray, meditate or just look back down at the stony yellow emptiness and ponder why this is all that's left of the might of Byzantium.

The locals find an unaccompanied foreigner puzzling. I haven't met another lone traveller in three weeks. 'Where is your wife?' 'Have you no friend?' 'Where is your family?' In restaurants and on street corners, in hotels and taxicabs, the questions are always the same. In Syria nobody is alone. They look at you as if you're some kind of gentle loon. Who will look after you in your old age? Explanations are by and large futile: hardly anybody speaks enough English or French to pass beyond the banalities.

I'm back in the courtyard of my hotel now, a gracious cloister hidden away behind a rough wooden door onto the lane outside.

Which is in turn hidden away inside the labyrinth of the Old City – which is spotlessly clean, unlike the world outside, where the rubbish lies so thick on the ground in some places that you seem to be driving through a rubbish dump. In Syria it's the interiors that are precious. The outside is not your responsibility. In here, though, in this world within a world within a world, beneath the bougainvillea, with the dusk call to prayer washing over me, it feels like a sort of paradise – as it's meant to.

⸺

If I could call a taxi and go to the airport now, this morning, I might well head for another city on the Silk Road: Alexandria. From Palmyra, caravans took the ivory, silk, porcelain and pepper down to Tyre, where they were loaded onto ships for the greatest Western hub of them all, named after the Greek who through his forays into Central Asia and India brought the Silk Road into being. Nowhere could be more Sotadic than Alexandria, incidentally: it was in Alexandria that Sotades wrote his most notoriously scurrilous poem on Ptolemy II's marriage to his own sister, Arsinoë, which led to his being locked up in a chest and thrown into the sea – poetry was taken seriously in those days. There's nothing much for the eye to see in Alexandria nowadays, I know that, whatever phantom city might lie hidden underneath the modern Arab sprawl, but a few years ago I was asked to review a book called *Alexandria: City of Memory* by Michael Haag and it filled me with a kind of longing that few books about great cities do – not just to go there, but to weave myself a richer life here, now. I could hardly wait to get into the Radio National studio to enthuse about it.

Alexandria

'When you are in love with one of its inhabitants,' Lawrence Durrell wrote in the *Alexandria Quartet*, 'a city can become a world.' He probably meant any city – and he was right about that, surely – but the city that famously became a world for Durrell was Alexandria . . . I was going to add 'in Egypt', but, for many of the foreigners who lived there (its Italians, Greeks, Jews, Syrians, even French and British inhabitants), at least in the nineteenth and first half of the twentieth century, Alexandria was hardly 'in Egypt' at all. According to Michael Haag, it was more a sort of Mediterranean city-state.

Founded by Alexander the Great (he laid it out – the streets and squares and temples – with grains of barley) it was strung out in Durrell's time along the seafront, still dreaming of the Ptolemies and Antony and Cleopatra, of the days two thousand years ago when it was at the heart of the Hellenistic world, swarming with artists, poets, theologians and thinkers, attracted to the city by the patronage of the Ptolemies, the days when it was the site of the Museion with its Great Library (a kind of open university, really, with lecture halls, laboratories, zoo and gardens), the very fountainhead of Western civilisation. In fact, Alexandria in its heyday a century ago seems to have dreamt of everything (Greece, Jerusalem, Paris, London, Rome) except what began on the other side of the lake hemming it in from the south: Egypt.

In the 1880s, an English visitor wrote that 'Alexandria is an Italian city; its vegetation is almost Italian; it has wild flowers. Its climate is almost Italian: it has wind and rain as well as fierce blue skies. Its streets are almost entirely Italian; and Italian is its staple language. Even its ruins are Roman.'

A few years later French became the lingua franca in Alexandria, at least amongst the monied classes – those who'd grown rich on the trade in cotton – the Greeks, Italians, Jews, and, of course, the British, who occupied Egypt for over fifty years, from 1882 until 1936, sending their sons home to Eton, Winchester and Sandhurst.

Durrell didn't say that when you are in love with one of its inhabitants, you fall in love with the city. He said it becomes a world for you. Durrell certainly didn't fall in love with Alexandria – there was little about modern Alexandria, the city that sprang up on the site of a small Arab village Napoleon found huddled by the sea that was lovable. It was a shambles. You could only love what it alluded to. 'I don't think you would like it,' Durrell wrote to his friend Henry Miller during the Second World War, after whetting Miller's appetite with salacious descriptions of Alexandrian women ('soft adze-cut lips and heavenly figures like line-drawings by a sexual Matisse'). 'I don't think you would like . . . this smashed up broken down shabby Neapolitan town, with its Levantine mounds of houses peeling in the sun . . . A sea flat dirty brown and waveless rubbing the port. Arabic, Coptic, Greek, Levant French; no music, no art, no real gaiety. A saturated middle european boredom laced with drink and Packards and beach-cabins. NO SUBJECT OF CONVERSATION EXCEPT MONEY.'

What Durrell loved (if loving is what he did) about the city he spent much of the war in (working in the British Information Office, writing propaganda) was the women: 'There's nothing lovelier and emptier than an Alexandrian girl,' he wrote. 'Their very emptiness is a caress.' The city sizzled with sex like a rasher of bacon, he said. He also loved the Greeks. 'The Greeks give our city noise and flair,' he wrote in his notebook. But the Greeks were only a minority amongst the foreigners (if highly visible). 'We are surrounded, impregnated with Jews,' he wrote, 'who give a curious flavour to the Alexandrian backcloth: a curious pessimistic hysteria, and a ceaseless "*conscience tourmentée*" . . . Tranquillity is poison to them'.

Two of his wives, of course, were Jewish.

Even worse than the Jews, from Durrell's point of view, were the Arabs.

One could hardly avoid them: after all, they made up two-thirds of the population, and many were more cultivated and better-read than he was. When he finally left Egypt for Rhodes after the war, he told Henry Miller that he felt 'like a crusader when I think of Egypt. I'd gladly put an army corps into the country and slaughter the lot of those bigoted, filthy, leprous bastards.' Michael Haag also more or less avoids the Arabs in *Alexandria: City of Memory*, but only because their memories are not what interests him here.

But the world Alexandria became for Durrell when he fell in love with Eve (Yvette) Cohen there (and dallied with many others) was what he called 'the spiritual city underlying the temporal one': the dream-city underpinning 'the rather commonplace little Mediterranean seaport which Alexandria seems to the uninitiated to be', as he put it. Well, what choice did he have? The temporal city (for him – since it wasn't Greece) was empty. He wasn't alone in this.

When E. M. Forster arrived in Alexandria during the First World War aged thirty-six – and Forster is the second of the three literary hooks Michael Haag hangs his wonderful book on – he was disappointed that it wasn't India. India was his spiritual home, as Greece was Durrell's – in fact, he'd already started writing *A Passage to India*.

Alexandria was a 'tousled, unsmartened sort of place', he wrote, admittedly with magical surroundings (the sea, the lake, the desert). But it wasn't the 'real East', he said, which 'always seems to be vanishing round the corner, fluttering the hem of a garment on the phantom of a smell'. Even after he'd done the Durrell thing and fallen in love, he wrote home to a friend in England, 'I cannot tell you how little I am interested in the Egyptians. Yesterday evening I dressed in civvies, and walked, as I do almost once a month, through the prostitutional and other quarters of the native town.

'It's such a meagre, vapid, attenuated East – nothing solid, no colour: non-European clothes and food, and non-European jabber: that's all . . .' These apparently rather dismissive words really just mean that Forster's erotic heartland lay elsewhere – 'erotic' in the broadest sense: lands that made him hungry for knowledge.

Yet, intriguingly, it was with an Arab, a tram conductor called Mohammed el Adl, whom Forster was by this time in love. Mohammed could do nothing to rescue Alexandria from its banality, but he could, and did, turn the city into a world for Forster, who went on to write one of the great guidebooks to Alexandria, the city that wasn't there.

Although he was an established writer in his mid-thirties by the time he went to Alexandria to work for the Red Cross, having published *Howards End, A Room with a View* and a number of other novels, Edward Morgan Forster had never had a sexual relationship with anyone and suffered from living with unsatisfied cravings he could not smother yet did not want to kill.

'I noticed you first in the spring of 1916,' he wrote to Mohammed el Adl (although not in a direct sense because Mohammed was dead by the time he wrote these lines to him), 'when I stopped with Furness [an old King's College friend of his] at Abou el Nawatir. You were on the Bacos tram which has the blue label. I, looking up from the ground as you went past, thought "nice", and the morning was fresh and sunny.'

So Forster (as one does) spent months waiting for trams – waiting for the right tram – the stops along the line becoming a line of poetry: Mazarita, Camp de César, Ibrahimiya, Cleopatra, Sidi Gaber . . . It took him these months of shy conversation, offering cigarettes, asking his name, before Mohammed finally said to him that he need not pay for a ticket on his tram.

Unfortunately Forster was caught by an inspector (ticketless), there was a scene, the conductor was blamed (because Forster was an Englishman) and threatened with the sack. So Forster, desperate at the thought of never seeing Mohammed again, asked him if they could meet. 'Any time, any place, any hour,' Mohammed said. And so they met, like any English courting couple, in the Municipal Gardens. Mohammed was just eighteen.

It was, by any standards, a fleeting affair – not even, perhaps, quite our notion of an affair at all. They saw each other as often as they could for some months, then Mohammed had to leave Alexandria, Forster went back to England, and Mohammed (now married) fell ill with tuberculosis. But it *was* love.

'I am very bad,' Mohammed wrote towards the end. 'I got nothing more to say. The family are good. My compliments to mother. My love to you. My love to you. My love to you. Do not forget your ever friend. Mohammed el Adl.'

Seven years after Mohammed's death, Forster wrote that marvellous letter to him from which I have just quoted. He told him about going back to Egypt after Mohammed had died – something he'd promised not to do.

> I'm glad I went back to Alexandria, I was happy there, and often thought of you, which I don't do now for months at a time, not even when I wear your ring. You have sunk into a *grande passion* – I knew you would, but you still float about the Egyptians for me – the complexion here, the stoop of the head there. It appears to me, looking back, that you were not deeply attached to me, excited and flattered at first, grateful afterwards – that's all. But if I am wrong, and if lovers can meet after death, and go on with their love, call to me and I'll come. I am close on 51 and I can never love anyone so much, and if there is the unlikely arrangement of a personal and pleasurable eternity, I would like to share it with you. I never have the sense that there is one, or that you are waiting for me, and I don't care for love as I did – my needs for the moment are lust and friendship, preferably but not necessarily

directed towards the same person. It is just the
chance, the faint chance: I am still just able to write
'you' instead of 'him' . . . I did love you and if love
is eternal I may start again. Only it's for you to start
me and to beckon. I knew how it would be from the
first, yet shouldn't have been so happy in Egypt this
autumn but for you, Mohammed el Adl – my love,
Morgan.

If it was a tram conductor who made the city not a place for Forster, but an experience (more like a verb, as it were, than a noun), it was the Greek poet Constantine Cavafy who revealed to Forster 'the spiritual city' that Durrell referred to, the city you couldn't see with your eyes, and made it possible for Forster to write his guidebook to a city of the mind. And it was of course Forster who did most to reveal Cavafy to the English-speaking world, publishing translations of his poems and essays about him in England – indeed this, not his own novels, was what he called 'the best thing I did'. Cavafy, Alexandria's most famous poet – more famous even than ancient Callimachus – is the third hook on which Haag hangs his book.

It was probably his King's College friend Robert Furness who first introduced them at the Mohammed Ali Club, a resplendent haunt of bankers, cotton brokers and rentiers in the centre of town – and at first Forster didn't quite know what to make of him: he was certainly 'sensitive, scholarly and acute', he wrote, 'and not at all devoid of creative power, but devoting it to rearranging and resuscitating the past'.

In time, naturally enough, as his Greek improved, his view of Cavafy deepened. Sitting with him in his cluttered flat on the rue Lepsius with its green, red and mauve walls, just above the brothel on the ground floor (the Greek Consulate has turned it into a museum), with Cavafy springing up and down to light candles and ply him with bread and cheese, Forster came to understand that Cavafy stood at a slight angle to the universe (as he put it). In Cavafy's poems about ancient Alexandria – as well as the squalor and seediness of the city he loitered and prowled in – one could hear (as Haag says) a voice that spoke across the centuries and from across another civilisation, the civilisation of the Greeks so often defeated, but in his person, in this far exile, neither broken nor extinguished. The civilisation he respected, Forster wrote, was a bastardy in which the Greek strain prevailed, and into which, age after age, outsiders would push, to modify and be modified. If the strain died out, never mind – it had done its work.

In other words, while inhabiting the Greek cafés, tavernas and pool-halls where he solicited young working-class Greeks for sex, the white-faced shop boys and sunburnt labourers, Cavafy also inhabited another city – a city of memories, a Greek city, one he could never leave, more real than the provincial tangle of lanes and avenues outside his windows. Cavafy was never interested in Egypt.

In the poem 'The City' he wrote:

> You tell yourself: I'll be gone
> To some other land, some other sea,
> To a city lovelier far than this
> Could ever have been or hoped to be . . .
>
> There's no new land, my friend, no
> New sea; for the city will follow you,
> In the same streets you'll wander endlessly.

After reading one of the essays Forster had written on Cavafy, the writer and critic John Middleton Murry remarked, with a very British edge to his words:

> In Alexandria Mr Forster has found a spiritual home. Being a dubious character, he goes off to a dubious city, to that portion of the inhabited world where there is most obviously a bend in the spiritual dimension, where the atmosphere is preternaturally keen and there is a lucid confusion of the categories. At this point a spinning eddy marks the convergence of two worlds, and in the vortex contradictions are reconciled. It is nothing less than a crack in the human universe. Mr Forster wanders off to put his ear to it. He finds Mr Cavafy already engaged in the enterprise.

Knowing Cavafy's poetry made it possible for Forster to write his guidebook to the city – reprinted in 1982, with an introduction by Lawrence Durrell, but still hard to find. It's remarkable because, unlike a Baedeker, for example, or a Lonely Planet guide, it doesn't describe what you can see, but what you can't see. It's a guide to memories, to what has disappeared, to what only exists in you.

My Lonely Planet guide, for instance, is unequivocal: 'There is little left of ancient Alexandria,' it says, 'the modern metropolis is built over or amongst the ruins of the great classical city . . . For the most part only an odd column or two or a gateway marks the location of legendary Ptolemaic or Roman edifices. Much of the romance of Alexandria lies in the past, not the present, and it's often a case of simply using our imagination.' And then it goes on to mention Pompey's Pillar (which it calls 'unimpressive' – and which in any case had nothing to do with Pompey, it's all that's left of the Serapium, where Cleopatra built her own great library), it recommends the recently discovered catacombs, the Graeco-Roman Museum, the Cavafy Museum, the zoo, the aquarium, but really it has to admit that what will haunt you is what you bring to Alexandria yourself.

Much of what haunted Cavafy and Forster was destroyed by the Christians – the people Forster calls 'spiritual thugs' – when Christianity became the official religion of the Roman world. All the same, when the Arab cavalrymen entered the city three centuries later in 642, they were so dazzled by the marble-clad buildings still gleaming in the sun that they had to shield their eyes. By the time Napoleon got there in 1798, it was just a fishing village with five thousand inhabitants.

In his guidebook Forster has you wandering aimlessly about the city, listening to him talk about what was, getting on and off trams, vividly recreating for yourself the vanished city. He hoped he'd written a guidebook you'd eventually not need, withdrawing into yourself and simply seeing the city without it. Durrell tramped around Alexandria ceaselessly with Forster's guidebook in his hand, trying to imagine what underlay the city he himself was beginning to evoke in its modern incarnation in his *Quartet* – the city at the end of its heyday – peopling it with Justine, Clea, Darley, Mountolive, Balthazar and all the other modern denizens of Alexandria. Only its Graeco-Roman past made Alexandria tolerable to Durrell.

Since the nationalists came to power in the 1950s, the cosmopolitan Alexandria has ceased to exist. Memory has largely died, drowned in a sea of Arabism and Islam.

What interests me in particular about Michael Haag's book is not so much the detailed accounts of what the city got up to during the two world wars – the influx of allied troops, the panic at Rommel's advance, the bombing raids, the murderous crush on the departing trains, the opulent parties, the society tennis matches (mixed doubles as usual), Noël Coward being thrown out of the Yacht Club for wearing shorts, and so on – this all has to be there, obviously, these wars were the two most tumultuous events in the city's life in recent times. Nor is it the gossip, although that, too, can be interesting: the parade of glamorous people who came and went – Toscanini, Pavlova, the stars of Italian and English opera, Elizabeth David, Daphne du Maurier (the place bored her stiff), the annual costume ball at Oswald and Josa Finney's (which finds its way into the *Alexandria Quartet*), and all the other shenanigans which the Rolls-Royce set got up to amongst their collections of Meissen, Persian carpets and French paintings, and indeed more louche surroundings, when it suited it.

Clearly the many pages on Lawrence Durrell's extraordinary life and the people and places he worked into his *Quartet* (in one form or another) are engrossing – not, I think, that he comes across as a very likeable man: he seems to have been (as one acquaintance told Haag) 'drunk three quarters of the time, a pretty boy, penniless', who wore the city like a cape tossed over his shoulders and made love to his vapid women as if they were Crème Chantilly. But then few of Haag's main characters come across as positively likeable, not even Cavafy, although there was something delicately raw about Forster that you can't help warming to.

But what will stay with me is the way Haag made me think carefully about what it is I miss in Australian, American or New Zealand cities – and I do miss something: there is no spiritual city. We regularly pay tribute to the Aboriginal owners of the land at public events, but I don't think many of us can go anywhere with those words. In any case, there were no Aboriginal cities. And this is a book that makes you think about cities: why some cities can mythologise themselves and others can't. I'm not sure it even has much to do with age – St Petersburg has done it brilliantly, for instance, although where it now stands there was nothing but a Finnish bog just three hundred years ago. It has something to do, surely, with whether or not there's a dream-city underlying the one we catch trams and buses in today. It's not a matter of museums and plaques – of knowing that Beethoven was born here or Byron had lunch there.

It has more to do, it seems to me, with the worlds (Durrell was right about that word) that you can unearth in your own consciousness as you sink into a city, worlds sparked very often by an instance of the city, such as Forster's Mohammed or Durrell's Eve.

And it's not just worlds of monuments but also of words, the sense of a city having been flooded over centuries with words in many languages about things that matter urgently. The Alexandrian poet Callimachus (much loved, by the way, by Cavafy, Forster and Durrell) put it perfectly:

> Someone told me, Heracleitus, of your end;
> and I wept, and thought how often you and I
> sank the sun with talking. Well! and now you lie
> antiquated ashes somewhere, Carian friend.
> But your nightingales, your songs, are living still –
> them the death that clutches all things cannot kill.

Alexandria – yes. A few days in Alexandria, if a magic carpet would fly me there, might be just the thing to make me avid to see what the eye can't see – but would I be up to it? For the moment, though, I am going nowhere. A quick dash to the bakery around the corner for fresh bread – otherwise I'll spend today in my tower. There is snow streaking the top of the mountain I stare at from my window and I am reminded that one of the reasons I write, and certainly how I write, has to do with snow. Ever since I read Donald Justice's poem 'Here in Katmandu', looking up at mountains topped with snow makes me think of why I write.

> We have climbed the mountain,
> There's nothing more to do.
> It is terrible to come down
> To the valley
> Where, amidst many flowers,
> One thinks of snow,
>
> As, formerly, amidst snow,
> Climbing the mountain,
> One thought of flowers,
> Tremulous, ruddy with dew,
> In the valley,
> One caught their scent coming down.
>
> It is difficult to adjust, once down,
> To the absence of snow.
> Clear days, from the valley,
> One looks up at the mountain.
> What else is there to do?
> Prayerwheels, flowers!

Let the flowers
Fade, the prayerwheels run down.
What have these to do
With us who have stood atop the snow
Atop the mountain,
Flags seen from the valley?

It might be possible to live in the valley,
To bury oneself among the flowers,
If one could forget the mountain,
How, setting out before dawn,
Blinded by snow,
One knew what to do.

Meanwhile it is not easy here in Katmandu,
Especially when to the valley
That wind which means snow
Elsewhere, but here means flowers,
Comes down,
As soon it must, from the mountain.

What I want to do is to write from my Kathmandu down here in the valley about being on top of the mountain in the snow.

    The snow: my snow is incidents from my imagined childhood – the bookshop where I worked, reading André Gide, meeting my mother for the first time, the multitude of kingdoms that the Bible conjured into being, the Berlin Wall, Venice, Corfu, Russia, Morocco, France, a string of infatuations, the passing caprice (although not the great love of my life, or only glancingly, not the pivot of my being) . . .

All these things are the snow I have thrilled to after climbing the mountain.

And then I have come down. To this day I vividly remember the sense of disenchantment that overtook me when we dropped below the snowline back into the untransfigured world on the way home from skiing trips when I was a teenager. The trees I saw through the window of the coach were now just trees, rocks just rocks and houses nothing but houses, whereas back up there in the snow every puddle, every leaf, every stone, every blade of grass, even our faces, had been magically transformed. Transported by the wonder of all that glittering whiteness, we now woke up to find ourselves back where we'd been before, tethered to all the usual, dun-coloured things of the country south of Canberra. It was as if we'd dreamt it all.

And so I write to recapture being up there in the snow. Partly I write about coming back down the mountain (every book is a kind of homecoming, wherever it might open – Cairo, Rome, Baden-Baden, Algiers, it doesn't matter), but mostly I write to imprint my Kathmandu with memories of snow.

It's important not to write from above the snowline, I think (although I pretend to sometimes, but that's just make-believe): above the snowline the thing to do is look. Besides, it's all been said – descriptions of snow are two a penny. After the wordless wonderment, it's time to wind back down the mountain, searching for the words. 'Tell all the Truth but tell it slant – / Success in Circuit lies'. That was Emily Dickinson's advice. 'The Truth's superb surprise,' she added, '. . . must dazzle gradually / Or every man be blind.'

Once back down in the valley, some of us scurry off to our towers to stifle our disillusion and re-enchant ourselves, picking over our memories like Emma Bovary when she got home from that ball at La Vaubyessard: a night of ambassadors and duchesses, actresses and poets, gleaming parquet floors, salons panelled with mirrors, tables covered in gold-fringed cloths, quadrilles, intrigues and illicit passions – and then suddenly she was home in Tostes! With her husband! (I spent two whole days last week reading *Madame Bovary*: not a patch on *Anna Karenina*, but I'm still drunk with it.) Others of us slink off to even more solitary hideaways in which to gird our loins – shacks on deserted beaches are favourites. Fernando Pessoa, on the other hand, although hardly gregarious by nature, takes up position in a more public sort of place.

> I see life as a roadside inn where I have to stay
> until the coach from the abyss pulls up . . . I don't
> know where it will take me because I don't know
> anything. I could see this inn as a prison, for I'm
> compelled to wait in it; I could see it as a social
> gathering-place, for it's here I meet others . . . I
> leave who will to stay shut up in their rooms . . .
> or to chat in the parlours . . . I'm sitting at the
> door, feasting my eyes and ears on the colours
> and sounds of the landscape, and I softly sing –
> for myself alone – wispy songs I compose while
> waiting.

I don't quite believe the 'for myself alone' bit, but, for all that, I have an inkling of what Pessoa might have meant: you sing your wispy song and others eavesdrop. Or pass on by – it's up to them.

What strikes me here is that even though he was no traveller (he barely left Lisbon in thirty years), Pessoa instinctively resorted to an image of the writer as a traveller at a wayside inn – an idle traveller, what's more, sunk in his own reflections on life and death and the passing parade.

One thing that Pessoa certainly knew a lot about was tedium – the desolation that comes not from having nothing to do (that's boredom, as he says), but from feeling that nothing is worth doing. Tedium for Pessoa is a kind of nausea: hunger with no desire to eat. It is to be conscious of not just the emptiness of the room you're in (that's boredom again), but, inescapably this time, the emptiness of the entire universe. Yet for Pessoa, sitting in the doorway of the roadside inn, there's no hint of either tedium or boredom. Here he is simply idling.

Now, when I gave the following talk at a travel conference in Melbourne, I hadn't dipped into *The Book of Disquiet* for over a year. Perhaps it's just as well: in their almost voluptuously self-pitying way, his reveries on the pointlessness of pretty well everything – from his own monotonous existence to the cosmos itself – could have sapped me of the desire to get up and say anything at all. Yet his acute awareness of the part boredom and tedium play in modern lives, bereft of any spiritual consciousness as they mostly are, has left its mark on me. His favouring of inner adventuring over mere travel across landscapes ('It's only within us that landscapes become landscapes') strikes me as wrong-headed – it shouldn't be a case of either/or – but I take his point, actually, about boredom being a kind of failure of the imagination. He'd doubtlessly have found me frivolous, but I like to think that if he'd been in that Melbourne audience he'd have thought that, in my fashion, I was onto something. What I was onto was that, in this postmodern era, it's boredom of one kind or another that pushes most people out the door and into a taxi to the airport – although to little avail, in my opinion. Look what happened to Emma Bovary when she took the coach to Rouen.

The Grand Illusion

'Life is first boredom, then fear,' the poet Philip Larkin wrote. Just having a bad day? Well, the American satirist Edward Gorey put it even more graphically: 'Life is intrinsically, well, boring and dangerous at the same time. At any given moment the floor may open up. Of course, it almost never does; that's what makes it so boring.' Thinkers and wits from Heidegger to Quentin Crisp have complained of much the same thing. Flaubert summed it up brilliantly: he calls the boredom that began to suffocate Emma Bovary once she was married 'that silent spider, spinning its web in the shadows in every corner of her heart'. (Significantly, the spider doesn't reappear until she's dead, her eyes dulling as if a spider had spun a web over them.)

Can they have been right? Is boredom, shot through with fear, really our default position as human beings?

Nobody *one would know* would ever admit to being bored, of course. We would all resort to more nuanced expressions.

A touch of 'ennui' is permissible, for instance, because it sounds Continental; and to complain of 'tedium', I think, hints at a rather elegant *taedium vitae* beneath the surface. But to confess to boredom is to admit to a lack of inner resources – or worse: it suggests that you may have a tedious, repetitive job or even none at all. Life might be humdrum, one might occasionally feel stale or tired ('weary' is better), but 'bored' sounds lower class or juvenile.

What most of us certainly are in the West these days – old, young, rich, poor – is aggressively domestic. Now, there is a price to pay for militant domesticity and the contentment it offers. Call it what you like – boredom, ennui, dullness – the price has to be paid. Until quite recently, in addition to the traditional remedies for this draining condition (sex, religion and carousing – and, more recently, fast cars), travel offered a reliable antidote to domesticity. Travel undermined habit. You didn't have to set out in search of Xanadu or El Dorado, you could go adventuring anywhere, your sails trembling in the wind as you headed for the horizon and uncharted seas. Not so very long ago I remember having a fabulous time in Adelaide. On one occasion I had a spectacular afternoon in Stoke-on-Trent. I loved Helsinki. From a train (moving trains being the perfect metaphor for the civilised self engaging safely with the wider world) even Manitoba looking interesting.

Like most Westerners, I still yearn to travel as an antidote to something fundamentally banal, if not boring, about my everyday existence. I am, however, almost always vaguely disappointed. These days I find it harder and harder to have a fabulous time – when I do anything, really, but *even* when I travel. Sex and religion, those time-honoured reasons for leaving home, have lost their urgency. For centuries, for example, in order to debauch themselves, the English travelled somewhere sultry, away from prying eyes. But these days, with good central heating and the collapse of moral principles, it's hardly worth the effort. The search for paradise in the post-Christian era seems pretty pointless as well. Clearly in certain zones paradise is still on offer: a sojourn in a land that time forgot, or at least where it's mangled, where nobody expects anything to happen apart from food poisoning, where there is no repetitious toil (for the traveller), where everything is beautiful, where the eye is delighted by vistas and prospects of loveliness. The food falls like manna, arranging itself in fantastic smorgasbords – chocolates fall magically onto your pillow every evening – and everything is clean. Sex, it's hinted, of a smiling, prelapsarian kind, might well offer itself here, too, almost unbidden, in hotel garden, nearby palm grove, or amongst the evening shadows on the beach. It's just like home, really, but better.

While all these things are briefly enjoyable in themselves, nowadays, as a package, the paradise being offered is just a game. The banality of our daily lives is not redeemed. Redemption is simply not something we still believe in with much conviction.

Perhaps my disenchantment is partly a question of age. As a friend in her seventies just back from a getaway tour of Chile put it, nothing seems *momentous* any more. Nice things can happen while you're away, but rarely anything transformingly beautiful. Everything feels like Devonport.

This is the Chateaubriand syndrome kicking in. This famous French writer and statesman once complained that once you've seen Niagara, there are no more waterfalls. Lamentably, although he died at eighty, he'd seen Niagara at the age of twenty-three, as half the population has these days. He was talking, I suppose, about the gradual disappearance of wonder from his life. Little by little it simply stops happening – wonder of the kind a Tuareg might feel when he first sees the sea, for instance, or I felt when I first saw a Tuareg. I'm trying to think of the last time I felt wonder – the sensation of being whisked out of time and space as I normally experience them, to be bathed in a sort of startling, epiphanic delight in something I don't understand and don't want to, not completely. I've felt interested, fascinated, enlivened, engrossed, delighted, frightened, blissful, amused, smitten, stupendously besotted (once), excited . . . but struck by wonder, the way I was decades ago when I entered a medina for the very first time or first saw Chartres Cathedral? It's not the phrase that springs to mind.

The travel industry does what it can to keep our hopes up. 'Fabulous' is the word they actually use over and over again in articles and advertisements for travel destinations, along with 'amazing' (not 'astonishing' – you'll be amazed but not astonished by Banff), 'unique', 'absolutely unique', 'exciting' and 'spectacular' – all code words for 'not boring', as your everyday life is presumed to be. (Actually, *it* isn't boring, I would like to suggest, whatever Larkin, Heidegger, Schopenhauer and all the others thought, *you* are – but we'll come to that.) Antarctica, Timbuktu, Uluru, Prague and the Mermaid Café in Kettering, Tasmania, are all 'fabulous', according to the weekend supplements. All offer 'escape' – from what? From a boring life, I take it. Or at the very least from a banal one.

Let me quote from the first paragraph of an article in a recent *Sunday Tasmanian* on Hastings Caves south of Hobart – it more or less distils the essence of what the modern traveller is presumed to be looking for: 'One of the Huon Valley's most spectacular natural adventure attractions . . . offers the amazing combination of a cave experience backed by the option of a dip in a warm spa pool.' Spectacle, adventure in the bosom of nature, amazement and, at the end of it all, blissful repose. What more could you want? If you're bored because your life is a meaningless, humdrum muddle, the Hastings Caves will send a bolt through you, making you feel alive again. If you're feeling more jaded than bored, constantly jostled by your busy life, stressed out, short of time, the Hastings Caves will give you time (in a soothing spa). They may even make time evaporate.

Travel, as the writers of this ad know, is about escaping from time *however we normally experience it*. And we normally experience it as waiting. We either wait for something to happen, for excitement (so go hang-gliding in the Hindu Kush) or we wait for things to stop happening, for relaxation (so head for Ubud to lounge by a pool and read absorbing trash). Which it is will depend on age, education and social milieu. Yet in the twenty-first century, for most of us, travel seems less and less likely to do the trick.

The industry, after all, rarely offers us anything but a form of infotainment, something our lives in the West are already saturated with. So travel tends to leave us feeling as if we'd never left our living room. You often arrive home with the impression you've spent two weeks watching repeats of *Spicks and Specks* – in fact, almost anything on ABC1 these days – or endlessly leafing through old copies of *Hello!* magazine. Modern transport makes it worse: as that arch-snob V. S. Naipaul has said (and, let's face it, we're all snobs to some extent, we all discriminate), 'Travel has become a plebeian, everyday matter, it has become a lower-class adventure.' It was, after all, the everyday that we were trying to escape in the first place. What is the point of venturing out into the world if it's full of people who are inured to the everyday – who think excitement is staying at a five-star hotel on the Gold Coast or visiting Disneyland? These are the people who dress up to the nines to travel economy class to Bangkok. They are just runaway slaves, soon to be recaptured.

The travel industry is focused on these runaway slaves, promising them small dramas of escape. Why wouldn't it be? They are easy to keep satisfied with short bursts of infotainment. In a world where heroic adventure in the old sense is virtually impossible, unless you climb Everest or sail solo around the world, why not promise the excitement of bungee-jumping, white river rafting, or camel riding in the Sahara? If love is out of the question, in other words, why not sell orgasms? In a world where everyone has seen everything, at least on the internet, show it to them again – plus food and shopping. Laugh as you do it, the way everyone laughs on ABC television, all the time. If you can get us laughing, we'll think we're having a Good Time. We'll hardly notice whether it's in Kyoto, Carcassonne or Casablanca and, unless we video it, certainly won't remember. Cacophonous emptiness is the postmodern condition. To transcend it through travel, we need a new approach.

André Gide, an enthusiastic traveller, once wrote in his diary, 'I've found the secret of my boredom in Rome. I don't find myself interesting here.' This was not a judgment on the art and ancient architecture of Rome, it was a perceptive comment on how boredom actually works. The place, the people, the sights are just what they are. Some are more likely to bring us to life than others, obviously, but ultimately the Birdsville pub, the Blue Mosque in Istanbul, Mount Everest, a Norwegian fjord, a lover's apartment in Brisbane, a Caribbean beach, Pompeii, the wilds of Borneo, Chadstone shopping centre, Machu Picchu . . . they are just what they are.

I am bored wherever I do not find myself interesting; wherever – being there, and being me – I feel not 'thickened' but, on the contrary, 'thinned out' by my experience. These are Gide's words. Talking about what made life good – or at least accorded it a banality of a superior kind – he proposed the idea of thinness and thickness: some things make you feel you're living a thick life, and other things leave you with the feeling that your life is thin. In his terms, it's not so much a matter of whether you experience life as empty or cluttered or boring or exciting, but of whether you experience it as thick or thin. Not deep, but dense.

Of course, I might *say* that I find Moose Jaw, Saskatchewan, as boring as golf, but really what I mean is that I don't find *myself* interesting in Moose Jaw. I bore myself in Moose Jaw. In Moose Jaw I feel thin. In grubby little Tozeur on the edge of the Sahara in Tunisia's south, however, where there's nothing to see and nothing ever happens, I feel dense with wakefulness. In Tozeur, in the labyrinth of the old town, lost amongst the endless palms, or just loitering with intent outside a carpet shop at night, when the town springs to life, I find myself very interesting indeed.

The antidote to boredom lies not in excitement, amazement, unparalleled vistas or repose in paradise, but in being woken up to our own inner complexity, our own density, and befriending it. Boredom, after all, is akin to loneliness. Where you travel to – it could even be Dubai – is not the point. Good travelling depends not on the travel, but on the traveller.

༄

Or, as Emily Dickinson (no rover, as we know) pithily put it: 'To shut our eyes is Travel.' Quite so – as long as you have an interior life to begin with. It takes courage to admit that it is not Noosa or Newcastle or even Paris that is boring, the week spent there strangely unsatisfying like Christmas in the bosom of the family, but you. In any case, if, to rephrase this thought in the words of Pessoa, 'the traveller is the journey' and 'what we see is not what we see but who we are', where does this leave the question of beauty, say, when we travel?

The idea of beauty is pivotal, I think, to why some of us travel and some of us don't. At its best, travel is being on the prowl, beholden to nobody, for the beautiful self we'd forgotten was locked up inside us. At home it can get buried under tired rituals, clichéd chatter and drudgery. We *can* prowl in the local supermarket, or even around our own bedroom, like Xavier de Maistre, who spent six weeks voyaging around his *chambre* (north, south, studying the furniture) and writing about it as if describing a tour of the Americas. (He much admired Laurence Sterne, who in turn loved Montaigne, so perhaps there was a faint echo of Montaigne in his tower here.) However, if the opportunity presents itself, for most of us it's more promising to try a little further from home.

'Beauty' is such a hackneyed word, applied to everything from Milford Sound to Kylie Minogue's bum, although, as I grow older, it's the only word I have to describe something fundamental to why I stay alive. When I was younger I was forever on the track of 'meaning'. I thought I'd have meaning more or less sorted out by the time I was twenty-two. Over time, though, I've pretty much given up on meaning. These days I am settling for beauty. It's not enough, of course, but it has to suffice.

I don't have in mind the purely picturesque, naturally. By 'beauty' I mean whatever kind of patterning makes us feel pleasurably raised to a higher power, to a higher pitch of being – and eager to reproduce the feeling. It could be the tango, Johnny Depp, high mass in Notre Dame, a face in a crowd, the smell of scones baking on a wintry afternoon – almost anything, really. What it is will depend on how we've lived – as I explained in this talk on beauty, first given in Melbourne's funky basement theatre fortyfivedownstairs to a warm, if argumentative, audience.

Beauty

A few days ago, walking by the water near where I live in Hobart, I had an experience that sums up much of what I want to say about 'beauty'. It was a beautiful day (bright, cloudy sky), with the inhuman, deep blue grandeur of Mount Wellington in the background (sublime, if you will), while in the foreground, between me and the mountain, the ripples on the water were grey and blue and green, looking like a painting, a painting I'd known all my life. Nestled cosily into the foothills above me, suburban Hobart stretched along the water (cottages, gardens, a café or two, people walking their dogs and fishing) and I felt momentarily transfigured. Can you picture it?

Now, do you remember the Rupert Brooke poem 'The Old Vicarage, Grantchester'? 'Just now the lilac is in bloom, / All before my little room' and so on – you must know at least bits of it. He wrote it in Berlin, dreaming of home, almost a century ago, when the world was in no better state than it is today. This is how it ends:

> Say, is there Beauty yet to find?
> And Certainty? and Quiet kind?
> Deep meadows yet, for to forget
> The lies, and truths, and pain? . . . oh! yet
> Stands the Church clock at ten to three?
> And is there honey still for tea?

Well, I can't speak with certainty for Certainty, or the Church clock or honey, although I will come back to them – or things very like them – but yes: Beauty is still there to find. And if the last four lines bring *Midsomer Murders* to mind, there's a good reason for that and for the show's popularity.

Indeed, eclipsed though it was in smart circles from about the time Brooke wrote that poem in a Berlin café in 1912 until just a few years ago, beauty is now back with a vengeance, even in smart circles. Suddenly, except on SBS, beauty is everywhere. The official French celebration of the millennium, for instance, was called, with some prescience, *La Beauté*. Books are being written on the subject, too, in growing numbers: Umberto Eco has written about it, as well as the Australian philosopher John Armstrong – even, in her fashion, Germaine Greer. The word is appearing in film titles (*American Beauty, Life is Beautiful* and others) and on Radio National not long ago I heard the American painter James McGrath say, 'I'm refusing to feel guilty about beauty.' For much of the hideous twentieth century one did feel guilty about it.

Why does beauty matter again, I wonder, as it did until about a century ago? Why has it re-emerged from behind the disfiguring mask of modernism? Well, it depends a bit on what you think it is.

I won't try to define it by cantering through Plato, Aquinas, Kant, all the modern theorists. Apart from anything else, I wouldn't be up to it. But I don't want to simply present a slide-show of images of Elizabeth Taylor (when young), the rose window in Notre Dame, Tutankhamen's death mask, the view from Lower Sandy Bay in Hobart and all those other things that so readily come to mind when we're contemplating the idea of beauty.

To talk sensibly about what beauty can mean, we need to remind ourselves that over the centuries – indeed, millennia – the debate about beauty has centred on whether it is an objective property of the thing we behold or a purely subjective response to form. In other words: is a rainbow lorikeet (or Audrey Hepburn, say, or . . . well, take your pick) simply unarguably beautiful or does it depend on who's looking? Or even when? Would the Dalai Lama, Bishop Desmond Tutu and the Queen all find Johnny Depp or Michelangelo's *David* beautiful? Would, indeed, I in five years' time, if I moved to Ghana tomorrow?

A popular approach has been to demonstrate that beauty is a matter of getting the proportions in objects and bodies right: a beautiful body is said to have a face one-tenth the length of the body, for instance; a beautiful column to be nine times as high as its diameter. Apparently we're programmed to point to such faces and say 'That's beautiful!' in whatever language we speak. Some think form (in order to be beautiful) must be married to function, others think it must mirror the divine. Taking a different approach, some evolutionary psychologists have proposed a genetic predisposition in human beings to call 'beautiful' whatever suggests fecundity: in bodies that would be whatever is good for breeding and in landscapes whatever is good for hunting – which doesn't quite explain Twiggy or a passion for sand dunes, let alone a Rothko painting or a Klee. There's rarely any point in arguing with evolutionary psychologists, though, so I'll just work my way around them.

If you have a mystical bent, you might see some sort of universal feng shui principle at work in my predilection for houses backed by a hill, overlooking water – something operating beyond anything I've been taught to appreciate. This sort of arrangement of the landscape certainly entrances me wherever I encounter it, from Wellington, New Zealand to Oporto in Portugal. It even figures in the secret land I invented as a child and wrote about in *A Mother's Disgrace*.

Now, those who think that beauty is in the eye of the beholder (the subjective school) have emphasised the almost infinite range of bodies or objects or scenes called 'beautiful' across time and space and cultures: from Venus de Milo to Jim Morrison and distended earlobes, from Brigitte Bardot to Arnold Schwarzenegger, from Botticelli to Cézanne or Cy Twombly's squiggles or Aboriginal dot paintings, from a Gregorian chant to Beethoven or 'Non, je ne regrette rien' (at least when sung by Edith Piaf: George Steiner, one of the world's leading minds on almost any subject, told me once, during an interview, that this is the piece of music that moves him most of all).

The word 'beauty', in other words, really does seem to mean different things to different people at different times in different places, *pace* all those theories about divine proportions and fecundity. It's confusing.

I think the whole debate about whether beauty is objective or subjective is largely beside the point. I think we can speak of beauty in ways that comfortably encompass both basic approaches. As I see it, if beauty is thought of as something that *happens* rather than as a property – something that happens to you and me and everyone, regardless of who we are or what is hardwired, or isn't, especially when our soul is twisted sharply by strong, opposing forces (calm and movement, chaos and harmony, peace and war, carnality and abstraction, adventure and cosiness, simplicity and intricacy – there's no end to the list of opposites that might twist your soul) then the way we use this word in English starts to make consistent sense.

To put it another way: I say you are beautiful when, paradoxically, *you embellish me* (my sense of a living self, my wholeness – something it's hard to hold on to at a time when everything is flying apart). Which is why we look askance at anyone who finds 'Que sera, sera' more beautiful than Beethoven's Fifth: if 'Que sera, sera' vividly embellishes your very sense of who you are, then just how deep, we wonder, is your sense of who you are? (George Steiner is allowed to find 'Non, je ne regrette rien' beautiful because he's George Steiner – he's already deep. You and I are not. He knows that.)

But back to the question of why beauty matters. Well, let me first speak about why beauty has mattered to me over the past ten or fifteen years – in particular since I started writing. It was suddenly vital to my will to survive that I magnify the beautiful wherever I encountered it – in faces, buildings, paintings, the sky, everywhere. I felt at that time dehumanised by disease (to put it bluntly), reduced to a body Picasso might have painted, and wanted to feel human again. Experiencing beauty is one of the most human things we can do. (Maybe chimps can do it – how would I know? But I doubt it.)

In *Night Letters*, the novel I began writing at that time, beauty comes in many guises, although I was unaware as I wrote of just how many: 'the people more beautiful than paintings' strolling past my exhausted narrator in Bologna; the scorch mark on the waiter Emilio's spotless shirt, making him 'beautiful' in the way a flawed Japanese tea-bowl is beautiful (and a flawless one isn't); sublime architectural vistas, such as the piazza in Vicenza at midnight, 'like a gaudy stage-set . . . opening up in front of me, drenched in amber light, heavily, sumptuously beautiful'.

At the very end of the novel, after visiting the Peggy Guggenheim museum in Venice (looking, significantly, at modernists – Magrittes, Mondrians and Pollocks, I now notice) and realising it was time I went 'home', I sit on the marble steps outside the museum beside the canal.

> Just across the canal from me to the right was one of the world's greatest sights: the extravagant pink confection of the Doge's Palace, the swarm of ferries and gondolas at the edge of the Piazzetta San Marco, the gleaming white loggia of the Marciana Library, the soaring red bulk of the campanile on St Mark's Square – bordering on the sublime, like an hallucination or bubble of memory, but curiously lifeless. Perhaps it was just my sombre mood. For an hour or so I gazed across at it but didn't see it. I could just as well have been at home, staring at my irises.

When I wrote those lines, I had no idea of what I was doing: opposing Magritte, Mondrian, museums, lifelessness and the sublime (on the one hand) to home and gardening on the other. It was quite unconscious. I feel now as if the Zeitgeist had tossed me a bouquet and I didn't quite know what to do with it. Yet it's at the heart of what it means to experience beauty, I now think.

The twentieth century was the century of the sublime – which I'm using today in the sense of awe-inspiring, almost crushing, like our Mount Wellington in Hobart. I don't mean 'sublime' as in sour-cherry cheesecake or Marlene Dietrich singing 'Falling in Love Again'. It was the century in which high art (although not always popular culture) often dehumanised its imagery and left us with a sublime wasteland of disembodied shapes. It was the century (at least as far as avant-garde art is concerned) of dissonance in music, the play of pure form in art and architecture, dazzling formal displays of linguistic juggling in literature and abstract, depersonalised literary theory – of an obsession with parts, not wholeness – as well as of the transformation of art lovers into consumers and citizens into taxpayers, not to speak of grosser acts of inhumanity and violent disembodiment, still with us.

In the West it was the century of Picasso, Dalí, Klee, Warhol, Beckett, Pinter, surrealism, Le Corbusier, Mies van der Rohe, Serra, Schoenberg, atonalists, constructivists, structuralists, abstractionists, minimalists – a multitude of ists, exciting every one of them, in his place (and it is an overwhelmingly male world, by the way) – indeed literally sublime. But 'beauty' tended not to be part of these men's vocabulary.

Here I was in Venice, retreating, instinctively, without even knowing I was doing it, from the sublime towards a different kind of beauty: the domestic (transfigured, of course) – home, irises – the embodiment of unremarkable, but utterly human feelings.

Subconsciously, by the way, I was embarrassed about it: many of the 'beautiful' passages in the book are in italics or put into somebody else's mouth. I'll tell you what I was doing: I was like those people who live in severely modernist houses – all plain white surfaces and sharp edges – who have an Amish quilt on the wall. So domestic, so homely, almost charming. They spotlight it – to show it up as an ornament they would otherwise not permit themselves.

The epitome of this homely kind of beauty in art is surely Pierre Bonnard (painting's Proust). If you're having problems bringing Bonnard's paintings to mind, let me remind you: a typical mature Bonnard might have a table with a few cakes on plates on it in the foreground; a nondescript dog sticking its head up to sniff at the cakes; a door and a window open onto a colourful, bourgeois garden, with a woman of no particular distinction doing something of no particular importance in it – picking something up, perhaps, or bending to look at something (it doesn't matter what). Or she may just be sitting in this unremarkable room, staring into space, doing nothing at all. Very often she's in the bath. It's middle class. It's feminine. It's dotted with craft (bowls and cups and flower arrangements). It's uncertain. It's intimate. *It's home*. There is no message, no doctrine. It's 'piddling', according to Picasso, who gave us his *Demoiselles d'Avignon* (shapes, not women) instead, and liable to slide into bourgeois charm or spiritual humbug.

Yet to me it's beautiful because it embellishes (deepens, vivifies, embodies, redeems, reveals in new colours, refracts) my own middle-class ordinariness, the everydayness of my actual life, making me feel luminous.

At this point let me remind you of another of Rupert Brooke's poems, written just before the dehumanised twentieth century took hold. It's called 'The Great Lover' and it begins on a rather lofty note, with Love and Death capitalised, with eagles, emperors and words such as 'godhead', 'splendour' and 'immortal' sprinkled about – verging on the sublime, in other words. And then, all of a sudden, at the beginning of the second stanza, we have this:

> These I have loved:
>   White plates and cups, clean-gleaming,

> Ringed with blue lines; and feathery, faery dust;
> Wet roofs, beneath the lamp-light; the strong crust
> Of friendly bread; and many-tasting food;
> Rainbows; and the blue bitter smoke of wood;
> And radiant raindrops couching in cool flowers;
> And flowers themselves, that sway through sunny
>   hours,
> Dreaming of moths that drink them under the moon;
> Then, the cool kindliness of sheets, that soon
> Smooth away trouble; and the rough male kiss
> Of blankets;

And on and on it goes: 'the good smell of old clothes' and 'new-peeled sticks; and shining pools on grass; /All these have been my loves.' It's vivid, fleeting, intimate, unabstract, common – it's home. Some of the final lines, however, make an important point about beauty:

> But the best I've known,
> Stays here, and changes, breaks, grows old, is blown
> About the winds of the world, and fades from brains
> Of living men, and dies.
> Nothing remains.

It is, of course, as any thoughts of beauty are, also a poem about bereavement, because beauty and bereavement go hand in hand.

Let me explain what I mean – there's nothing maudlin about it. When we see something or someone beautiful (to our eyes), we are embellished or transfigured – made newly whole, whole in a new way – by what we see or hear. It usually *is* a matter of either seeing or hearing, although obviously Proust was turned inside out by tasting his madeleine, and smells also have their aficionados: in his recent book *The Secret of Scent*, Luca Turin likens a certain French perfume, Nombre Noir, to rose and violet against the almost saintly background of cigar-box cedar. The voice of the perfume, he said, was that of a 'child older than its years, at once fresh, husky, modulated and faintly capricious. It brought to mind a purple ink to write love-letters with, and that wonderful French word *farouche*, which can mean either shy or fierce or a bit of both.' He really liked this fragrance. But usually, as I say, it's a matter of seeing or hearing.

Now, what *happens* as we look and listen seems almost always connected to a desire to reach out and hold and to experience again, even as we know there must come an end to what we're experiencing. At the most trivial or vulgar level, it's the almost unbearable joy we might feel while watching the ball scene, for example, in Prokofiev's *Romeo and Juliet*: you want to drown in it, you want time to stop, you want the heart-wrenching beauty of the music and the dance to go on forever, but it must end, and it must end now or else you'll ignite and burn to a cinder. We are wrenched between holding on and letting go forever. This is what twists our soul. Beautiful.

In *Corfu* I put it a little differently: my narrator (is it me?) is contemplating the puzzling sentence in Tolstoy's *Anna Karenina* where Vronsky, having just seduced Anna after a year's blandishments, 'felt what a murderer must feel when he looks at the body he has robbed of life'. In knowing beauty, I wrote,

> seizing it . . . and knowing it with a fierceness that leaves you unconscious of whether you have been ravishing beauty or been ravished by it, you must

entertain bereavement. A poem, an orchid, a sky, a Daphnis, a Chloe – it doesn't matter what or whom you seize, for the instant you stretch out your hand to touch it, you hear the whisper: *This will die.*

Not the poem or orchid, not the beloved – not this Daphnis or this Chloe – but this *particular* moment of enchantment, this *particular* experience of the orchid's or Chloe's beauty. We fear that the beauty that is making us feel so alive might prove to be nothing but what it seems . . . Where there was a living body, so to speak . . . we fear we might soon wake to find a corpse . . . Beauty and mourning . . . go hand in hand. Tolstoy got it exactly right.

There is a memorable episode in Forster's *A Passage to India* that captures beauty's pathos – and the twist to our soul – to perfection. It's particularly affecting – and wrenching – because, for all its high seriousness, the tone is gently mocking. The Muhammadan Dr Aziz, in bed with a slight fever in his 'squalid bedroom', is surrounded by well-wishers who have fallen to bickering and gossiping amongst themselves. Apropos of nothing at all, Dr Aziz holds up his hand, calling for hush, his eyes begin to glow and 'his heart to fill with tenderness'. He recites a ghazal by the celebrated Urdu love poet Mirza Ghalib. Everyone is deeply touched – even the police inspector, the engineer and the engineer's schoolboy nephew – because pathos is 'the highest quality in art' and the poem compared mankind to flowers, as poems should. Dr Aziz sang 'sadly, because all beauty is sad'. The poem, 'a breath from the divine lips of beauty', was also 'a nightingale between two worlds of dust'. And it left Dr Aziz in his lonely squalor feeling at one with India and thinking quite intensely about women, as poetry often did in his case.

Now, I admit that this notion of beauty as the experience of the transfiguration of the ordinary in us – the bringing to the surface of appetites, fantasies, deep structures of the self, 'the image of our soul made perfect', as Plotinus put it (so beautifully) – I admit that this notion has its dangers. It can leave us with overrefined sensibilities, a sort of narcissism, perhaps, even an ineffectual dandyism. It can lead to a kind of decadence, to a passion for altered states. Or at the level of the trite, it can lead to *Midsomer Murders*. At that point the barbarians can sweep in and take over. You have to be on your guard.

May I, in conclusion, read you again my opening words about what I felt looking back across Lower Sandy Bay from the point?

> It was a beautiful day (bright, cloudy sky), with the inhuman, deep-blue grandeur of Mount Wellington in the background (sublime, if you will), while in the foreground, between me and the mountain, the ripples on the water were grey and blue and green, looking like a painting, a painting I'd known all my life. Nestled cosily into the foothills above me, suburban Hobart stretched along the water (cottages, gardens, a café or two, people walking their dogs and fishing) and I felt momentarily transfigured.

You can see what I meant now, I hope. I meant that the shards of my memory of who I fundamentally am have been kaleidoscoped by Lower Sandy Bay into a revealing new mosaic. That's beauty.

So, if you want to have a good life – *une belle vie*, as the French say more perceptively, voting for beauty over virtue – it's best to start early. For beauty to strike, you have to have some shards to kaleidoscope. (Does that sound elitist? Only if you think that the shards I value are solely splinters of high culture. Which is far from being the case.)

'Kaleidoscope' – I overuse some words, I know that. 'Zigzag' and 'spiral', for example – words that bend straight lines into new shapes. Mazy, meandering words are the sort I like – coils and corkscrews, loops and labyrinths. And arabesques, naturally. Straight lines are death: the arrow is fired, it hits the target – the end.

I began zigzagging and meandering when I was still a small boy on walks with my dog in the late afternoon. Talking to myself in my secret language (and to the dog in Russian), I'd roam the streets around our house, in and out of side streets, across gullies, through parks, along the river, with no aim but the pleasure of the ramble. While other children played cricket on the road outside their houses or did their homework, I looped for miles around the bungalow-lined streets of our hilly neighbourhood, with just my fox terrier for company. (It's strange: I rarely see children walking their dogs any more. Why not?)

Apart from exercising the dog, I was learning to map. Bit by bit, I was turning topographical. Half a century later there's little need to be topographical, what with Google Earth and all our other navigational aids, but I am still a map person. I collect maps, study maps, draw maps, love maps. I often sit over lunch with an atlas lying open on the table beside my plate – wherever it falls open, I study it. Today it was Jordan. Cities, countries, medieval *mappae mundi*, my *Times Atlas of the Bible* – I'll pore over a map of anywhere. It may be a pointless pleasure (like many of my other pleasures), but it's a pleasure nonetheless. If I had to choose this instant between an hour spent reading a street directory and an hour spent reading Tolstoy, I'd almost certainly choose the street directory. Every page is reliably thrilling. Even my humble clipboard is a pink and green street map of Florence.

At some level, Milly Molly Mandy is to blame. And William. There was always a map of the village, just inside the front cover. The vicarage, the lolly shop, the post office, the wood, the fields, all the cottages . . . or at least, that's as I remember them. I felt immediately gathered in when I saw these maps, part of the family, eager for a story. That's why books with passages about The Man walking along The Street in The City – all that Borgesian flimflam – leave me cold. Which street? Which city? Sargento Cabral in Buenos Aires? General López in Santa Fe? Tell me! Not that I've been to either place – but I'll go there if given directions. And wait on tenterhooks to see what happens next.

When I started writing, drawing my readers into a specific place at a specific time was naturally important to me. *A Mother's Disgrace*, my first book, an autobiography, opens in a particular café, Groppi's, on the Midan Talaat Harb in Cairo. I even provided photographs of Lane Cove on Sydney's north shore, where I grew up, of Martin Place in Sydney in about 1950 (taken by one of those street photographers we no longer need – like atlases), of Moscow University, where I went to study in the 1960s, and other faces and places that figure in the book. Many writers (everyone from Tolstoy and V. S. Naipaul to the woman next door) start with autobiography in some form or other – with 'home' (that nest of experiences and feelings we think of as embodying who we are) – indeed sometimes they even begin with something cruder than 'home': they begin with 'house'. (I have a picture of *my* childhood house printed in *A Mother's Disgrace*.) But eventually you have to get out of the house – out of autobiography – because its walls are so smooth with constant use that they've become mirrors, leaving us being just us (ironing, shopping, falling in and out of love, going up and down staircases, feeding the canary). *We*, you see – the unmediated *we* – are not beautiful. I don't mean as Juliette Binoche or – whom shall I choose? – Alain Delon, let's say, when he was young, are beautiful, but beautiful to behold because of a transfigured wholeness.

Night Letters pretends to move on from autobiography, it pretends to be a novel, but it, too, begins (after a page or two of geographical game-playing and a map to peruse inside the front cover) in a well-known surgery on Elgin Street in Carlton, Melbourne. The pasta shop just around the corner, which I mention at one point of high emotion, is still there. *Corfu* opens on a platform at Roma Termini; *Twilight of Love* on that train pulling into Baden-Baden railway station; *Arabesques* in the casbah in Algiers. I leave a few of the details hazy as a rule – not all but some, especially exact times and distances – one doesn't want to stifle readers' imagination or make them feel stuck at home. On the other hand, I don't want them blowing about the sky like escaped balloons. I like a bit of tethering.

It's not exactly the height of sophistication, this business with maps, photographs and recognisable railway stations, but it's how my imagination works: I see someone, real or imagined, in a particular place on a particular occasion and want to spiral out and up from that man on that day in that place on an updraft of stories – well, of gossip, really, as I've said. In my last book I couldn't resist including a large map of Europe and North Africa together with a coloured photograph of almost everything I mentioned, from the casbah in Algiers at the beginning to the windows of Paris at the end.

There are more subtle techniques for evoking place, though. Homer uses repetition – with slight variations – to evoke landscapes: think of the 'wine-dark sea' and 'dawn's roseate tentacles', which recur (it can sometimes seem) every few pages.

And so in *Corfu*, for instance, it's not through laziness that I refer again and again to the 'crest' above the house my main character lived in, which he crossed and dipped down to the sea from – I refer to the 'hilltop' and the 'ridge' as well, but I like to repeat key words: I want my reader to feel anchored somewhere not necessarily real (although it is), but familiar, to feel at home there, as I did in Milly Molly Mandy's village. In fact, when the translator tried to use synonyms in French for my repetitions, I said, 'No, use the same word – repeat yourself.' The French get very touchy about this – in French a masterful writer always finds a different word. Flaubert, for example, never used a word twice on the same page.

Of course, Homer also has patches of descriptive density: a sudden detailed description of a gateway or feasting hall, say, or of a skirt or wood – but the key to evoking place in the reader's mind, I am convinced, lies in sprinkling the pages with references to just a few key features (smells, colours, textures, one house, one hill) and leaving the rest to the reader's imagination – anchoring it, but not walling it in. 'You know, you got Adelaide just right,' all sorts of people have said to me after reading *Corfu*. In reality, all I did was sketch in a few details (flatness, a jetty, *Brigadoon* in church halls), like a post-impressionist painter such as Dufy or Matisse. The rest they filled in for themselves and so naturally they find the picture true to life. Easier to do with Adelaide than Irkutsk, of course, but even with Irkutsk you have to trust your readers' own imaginations.

The point is that I want your *complicity* in my enterprise, I want you to join me in telling the story. That's why I always shy away from mentioning anything too numerical – exactly how many years ago something happened, precisely how many kilometres away and so on. While I like to be specific about the era and the place in order to fire up your imagination, I steer clear of exact measurements, so it can waft. I'll describe a character as 'tall' or 'short', but never as five foot eleven. The poet Paul Valéry famously said he could never bring himself to write the sentence: 'The marchioness went out at five o'clock.' (*La marquise sortit à cinq heures.*) I sympathise. Regardless of when she actually went out – and in art a marchioness would be well advised to go out mid-morning or at nightfall – a marchioness, aesthetically speaking, should be above numerals. Their punctuality is to be taken for granted. There are no marchionesses in my books, but I long ago noticed my own Valéry-like reluctance to mention specific numerals: what I like is 'dozens', 'hundreds', 'half a century', 'straight after the war', 'after breakfast', 'a couple of weeks later' and so forth (and I also like 'and so forth'), because otherwise it sounds like a police report. Police reports may often be fiction, but they are rarely art.

The important thing, in other words, if you want modern readers to accompany you on a journey somewhere, is not a detailed photographic survey of a place, with mention of the dozens of dishes on offer in its restaurants (a spot of teriyaki sauce on the tablecloth tells you all you need to know) or every variety of tree to be found in its parks (a cypress and a holm oak and you've got Corfu). It's the rhythm of the constituent parts that's telling, it's the brushstrokes, with one or two buildings described in great detail, like one of Matisse's rugs. That should be all you need to draw your reader after you, imagination on full alert, picturing how these articulated spaces are filled. Turgenev and Flaubert would have disagreed, as would the painters of their time – our complicity as readers was probably not what they were aiming for – but by Chekhov's time things were changing, in prose and in art: a Pomeranian, a beret, grey eyes, a watermelon, air so still and warm you can hardly breathe – not much more – and you know all you need to know about the lady with the little dog and Yalta and why this man and this woman would fall in love; a wash of blue and purple, a white streak just offshore, a couple of reddish blobs outlined in black on the beach and you have *The Mediterranean* by Raoul Dufy. In just a few years our way of seeing the world through art changed – became more Japanese, actually, more woodcut-like. I'm not sure why. Was it the flowering of photography? Reading *Madame Bovary* I couldn't help feeling that Flaubert didn't trust me: I enter a room with him and he describes every splinter of wood, every speck of dust and how the light falls on it. I can see why autocrats like realists: they don't trust us, either. Modern readers like to be provoked into seeing and feeling for themselves.

It's true that there are some contemporary writers, such as Nicholson Baker and Don DeLillo, as well as a few photographers, whose very trademark is the flattening out of the picture they're painting through a wealth of undifferentiated detail. It's not that they don't trust us, though: they are imparting a vision of the world. I am rarely seduced.

After thinking aloud along these lines at the Byron Bay Writers Festival a few years ago – you see, I can't bring myself to name the year – at a session on the dreaded subject of 'Spirit of Place' (a phrase that usually turns my mind completely blank), I offered the audience a postcard from Byron, written the previous afternoon on a sandhill facing the surf. Byron Bay is desperate to be loved. Sydney, big-bosomed and brassy, is not: love me, she says, hate me, I don't give a stuff; and Melbourne, being a trifle tonier and knowing she's got class, sniffs: if you don't love me, then you simply have no taste. But Byron Bay, like a new puppy, is always asking, 'Do you love me? Aren't I beautiful? You love me, don't you?' And so I chose the words on my postcard carefully. Written at five-fifteen in Byron Bay, it was unavoidably alliterative.

> It's green, of course,
> and gold – a wheaten gold, nothing too brassy –
> and BLUE, overwhelmingly BLUE:
> blue-greens and aquamarines
> and cobalts and misty mauves . . . but BLUE.
> And when it's NOT blue,
> I want to walk to where the blue is pounding
> and drown in blue.
> There's a jolting whiff in the air of brawny
>   Neptune
> rising from the brine.
>
> Along the waterfront (ritz and trash)
> I can also smell money and perfumes from Paris.

At certain times, though, on certain corners,
I could swear Poison by Dior has turned into
   patchouli oil,
and the satins here and there have ragged edges.
The Toorak hairdos, too, are falling out of shape,
ending up as dreadlocks and tresses with split ends.
I think the Great Uncoiffed are gathering,
dreaming dreams of being loved,
and stretching time, a little more, a little more . . .
   until it pops.

Nature has been tamed appealingly in Byron Bay.
Yet, in those copses and pretty grey-green swamps,
I get the feeling fires might on certain nights be lit
and painted bodies might indulge in quite
   unchristian
(hardly even Buddhist) rituals.
Perhaps not, perhaps that's just the little pagan elf
   inside me squawking,
asking to be let out instantly to frolic in its funny
   hat.
(And why not?)

Byron Bay is forever leaning out as far as it can
   (without falling smack on its face)
towards the east, towards the ball of molten gold
that swims up into the sky each morning from
   South America.
Leaning, leaning . . .

Having super time –
is the dog's rash better? –
wish you were here.

Love,
Me

Did I capture something about Byron Bay with these broad strokes, I wonder?

The idea of 'capturing' is something that fascinates me. It's so primitive a metaphor, yet something about it cuts to the heart of what it feels like to create an image. What does a camera 'capture'? A painter? A writer? An autobiographer?

What the autobiographer captures (and I should know) – and perhaps the self-portraitist as well – is the flash of intimate electricity between two poles: what is true about what we are (the concealed mirror in most self-portraits) and how at this moment, as we recount or paint ourselves, we would like to be remembered (even by ourselves) at the hour of our death. In the portrait of his own childhood, called *Words* in English, Jean-Paul Sartre talked about *becoming his own obituary*. André Gide, too, whose *Journals* record in dazzling detail his entire life from his teenage years almost until his death, said, 'Our whole life is spent in sketching an indelible portrait of ourselves . . . We recount our lives and lie to ourselves, but our *life* will not lie, *it* will tell the story of our soul.' What is exciting is the almost erotic current set-up between the two. When you look at Derain's self-portrait, for instance, a fauvist masterpiece, you know that the zigzagging face, the slashes and blocks of brilliant colour are not what Derain saw in the mirror as he painted, and the difference excites us. All great portraits, surely, play games with the mirror.

While sitting silently for my portrait, staring straight ahead, afraid even to twitch, practically hallucinating, I became almost obsessed with the question of what sort of likeness the painter captures and how he does it. In fact, a good portrait painter captures more than a likeness, but it's hard to find the words for exactly what it is. A good portrait has an almost occult presence. As Dorian Gray said, 'There is something fatal about a portrait. It has a life of its own.'

Oddly enough, it's not a subject many people have written about in any depth. They write about van Dyck's portraits or David Bailey's photographic portraits, but not so often about portraiture in general. And almost never about what it *feels* like to sit for your portrait. So, when I came to speak at the National Portrait Gallery in Canberra, where the portrait in question had just been hung, about what I think an artist captures, my remarks mostly grew out of the extraordinary experience of sitting. Over the years since then, I've given a version of this talk in several cities and galleries, but, because of the way my mind works, I always begin in a particular place (the National Portrait Gallery) in a particular city (London) and then come home.

Caught You!
Reflections on Being Painted

They were all there: Elton John, French and Saunders and Stephen Hawking (naturally). Even the Queen was there, smiling at nobody in particular. Celebrities everywhere I looked, really; all instantly recognisable (apart from David Bowie), even two rooms away, half-hidden by women in hats. (To be frank, Bowie's face, which can look so fetching in a certain light, looked like a patch of snow splashed with pig swill.)

'That's that writer – whatshername,' said the man in front of me, with a discreet nod at the face he'd just caught sight of across the room.

'Who?' His companion needed to know instantly.

'Margaret Drabble's sister.'

'A. S. Byatt?'

'Yes.'

'No, it's not.'

'Yes, it is.'

'No, it's not – the mouth's all wrong.'

'*Exactly*.'

I drifted across to it, peered at the squiggly mess of mauves and blues and reds and whites, stepped back an inch or two, chuckled to myself and thought: yes, that's her all right, down to a T. He's caught her exactly.

I glanced around to see who I might share this moment of recognition with, but nobody was looking. I wanted to exchange a complicit smile with somebody – anybody, really, the way you do at a sideshow when the illusionist reaches over and pulls an egg out of your ear. All around me little knots of visitors – couples for the most part, but there was the odd threesome and family group – were stopping in front of portraits of the famous to point, make faces, chortle, comment and move on. Occasionally there'd be a burst of laughter. What I wanted to do was to connive with somebody at something I'd just seen.

But what had I seen, exactly? What was it I wanted to connive at?

And, if sleight of hand was involved, who was tricking whom? Was the artist making a fool of A. S. Byatt or she of him? Or both of them of me?

It's amazing. We live in an era when the world is awash as never before with images of human faces and bodies. From the moment we open the newspaper over breakfast to the moment we switch off the television at night, we are inundated with lifelike images in their thousands. We can summon them up at will in ways undreamt-of just decades ago. We can create them ourselves in a split second by pressing a button. Yet, astonishingly, the rooms and corridors of this portrait gallery still felt haunted in a way a cinema, or even my living room with its television screen in one corner and pile of magazines on the coffee table, never does. Sometimes, for just a split second, as I turn away from a canvas, in that infinitesimal moment before what I have just been looking at becomes a memory, I have the sensation of frozen life unfreezing on the wall behind me. How can this be? What is the power of the painted portrait?

I flee to the comforts of the basement café to consider the whiff of voodoo (in which I do not believe) in the halls above.

⁓

The hocus-pocus first makes itself felt when we open our mouths and say, 'There's Nick Cave!' or 'That's Kylie!' or 'Isn't that Lionel Murphy?' Well, no, it's not. It's actually dabs of pigment on a piece of stretched canvas. (Or it used to be – the media have changed with the class of sitter: virtue still gets oil and canvas, while mere fame gets whatever comes to hand – a spray can in Nick Cave's case, a camera, fittingly, in Kylie Minogue's.) Nevertheless, just as we say, 'The magician pulled an egg out of my ear,' knowing he's done nothing of the kind, we all say, without reflecting, 'That's Lionel Murphy.'

And we've got a point. For tens of thousands of years humans have believed that images capture more than just a likeness, especially images physically created by an artisan's hands – figurines, effigies, dolls and painted portraits: they capture a living self. (Photographs, on the other hand, or movies and videos, created by a little box, as a rule remain just likenesses, however striking.) It's the sort of quaint superstition we thrill to in backward tribespeople in television documentaries, but imagine we ourselves have left far behind. Well, we have and we haven't, and that's partly why portraits still provide a frisson mere pictures of people don't. The suspicion that an artist can capture more than a likeness lingers in every carved idol, in every Russian icon with its propensity for wonder-working and every St Christopher medal dangling from rear-vision mirrors in taxis all over the world.

We've come a long way, obviously, in Carlton and Balmain from the days when people believed that matter could be infused with spirit, so that you could take possession of somebody's essence, for example, simply by cutting off his head and gobbling up his 'power'. But, having been 'headhunted' myself, as it were (having sat for a portrait), I suspect we haven't come quite as far as we think. In fact, if the Yale psychologist Paul Bloom is right, to believe in a captured essence of some kind *inside* physical objects is part of being human – whatever our reason might tell us. It's an evolutionary adaptation. Just ask yourself, as he suggests to his readers in his book *How Pleasure Works*, how you would feel about wearing one of Hitler's cardigans, for instance. Uncomfortable? Why? Or how would you feel when you found out (as poor Goering did about his Vermeer) that your Picasso had not been painted by Picasso. Would you find it just as beautiful? The evidence is that you would not. Goering, I can tell you now, was not at all pleased.

In a word, if Bloom is right, our subconscious hasn't quite kept up with our reason. Certainly, as I sat being stared at in Robert Hannaford's studio in Adelaide a few years ago, ancient anxieties about bodies and selves unexpectedly bubbled to the surface. It was a deeply unsettling experience. Perhaps 'headhunted' is putting it a little too forcefully. Robert Hannaford once sat next to me in a plane, and after he'd asked me if I was David Marr and I'd said no, we lapsed into silence. He sketched. A few weeks later he sent me the sketches, explained the mix-up and invited me to sit for my portrait. It would take a good week, he said. I thought that this could prove to be a week unlike any other I'd ever had, so I said yes.

The first few hours of the first sitting were like a séance in some shaman's tent. While the artist roamed the room, squinting at me back-to-front in a hand-mirror and staring into my eyes from the end of my nose; while he paced, wheeled, hummed, smiled, glared and stood stock-still, I sat in a chair looking straight ahead. Was he casting spells? I cocked my head slightly to the left, then slightly to the right, moved a knee, shifted a foot, clasped and unclasped my hands, but mostly just sat back in my chair, my legs stretched out in front of me, performing myself in silence as the wintry light from the window grew brighter towards noon. (I was even provided with a little platform to perform myself on – you can see it in the painting. It's a deft postmodern touch, like including the lights and make-up kit in a photographer's portrait.)

Right beside me, level with my face so I couldn't see it without turning my head, was the blank canvas.

Suddenly, at midday, Robert grabbed a stick of charcoal, bolted across to the canvas and began sketching – looking, sketching, stepping back, darting forwards, sketching, looking, peering, looking, sketching . . . and in ten minutes it was over.

Striding across to the far wall, where there was another mirror for him to peer back at us in, he swivelled, stared at us, then smiled. Yes, apparently there were now two of me, side by side.

I climbed down from my platform and turned to look. I was thunderstruck. In just a few strokes of charcoal he'd caught me. A squiggle or two on a piece of canvas and there I was: a motionless black-and-white me, as spare as one of Calder's wire sculptures. I didn't even have eyes or a mouth, but it was another me and nobody else in the universe. I laughed. I felt as if I had been robbed of something in broad daylight.

Over the next week or ten days Robert Hannaford prised an ever more nuanced self out of me, a self with feelings, with heightened self-awareness, a self with a past (the key, according to Paul Bloom, to the illusion of essence) and applied it in dabs as thin as gold leaf to the canvas beside me. A self, not just a likeness. At least, that's how it felt. It felt like sorcery, although I know it was only magic.

Robert Hannaford, needless to say, denied any involvement in the art of sorcery – or even magic. 'I just paint what I see,' he said, ever the naturalist. Elsewhere he has claimed that his hand paints what his eye sees, as if there were not only no 'I' to capture, but no 'I' to do the capturing. Towards the end of the process, when I asked him what sort of man he saw in front of him, he refused even to answer the question. 'To answer that, I'd have to use the other side of my brain,' he said. I didn't believe him then and don't now.

These days, in this era of genomes and stem cells on the one hand and the postmodern collapse of any belief in an integrated self on the other ('I' being just a linguistic convenience to get us through the day in one piece), these notions of mine of a represented self are an embarrassment – and any belief in transferred traces of a being simply primitive gibberish. After all, we now know that there's nobody there to represent or transfer.

Portraits such as Stephen Finer's of David Bowie, for example, in the National Portrait Gallery in London – a splash of bruised, mauvish hues on white – cocks a very brash snook indeed at the notion of capturing anything at all: dream any dream you wish of 'David Bowie', Finer seems to be saying, the paint on my canvas is beside the point, except as a kind of talisman to focus the mind.

Andy Warhol's four silk-screen prints of Elizabeth II in the same gallery mock the idea of captured essences from a different angle: there is no 'Elizabeth II', these brilliantly banal likenesses in pinks and blues announce with a sneer – or at least none of any interest to Warhol – whatever ideas pass through the head of that woman at Windsor Castle when she first wakes up in the morning. 'The Queen' is nothing more than an accumulation of images, a series of representations of representations.

Psychologists, philosophers, physicians, Marxists, post-modernists, sociologists, geneticists, even the odd theologian all seem to agree: there is no self. Can I be blamed for smiling, then, when I think I've glimpsed one, caught on canvas?

What sort of self do I think I've seen? One of my artist friends in Melbourne says that when he draws a face he draws the face *plus* something else. By 'self', though, I mean more than this. Richard Brilliant, in his detailed study of the art of portrait painting (*Portraiture,* first published in 1991), argues that there are five 'essential constituents of a person's identity': a recognisable appearance; a name belonging to nobody else; a social role; self-performance like nobody else's; and a consciousness of not being other people. I wonder, however, if even Brilliant's 'identity' quite covers what I have in mind when I speak of a 'captured self'.

It's true, for example, that in the photographer Napoleon Sarony's 1882 portrait of Oscar Wilde in the National Portrait Gallery in London we recognise this body as 'Oscar Wilde' (or 'Oscar Wilde's', if you're feeling mystical); this name and no other springs to our lips when we see the photograph; his known function as artist (if not specifically as writer) and aesthete are strongly suggested; his foppish character is captured exactly in the pose (and the hose); and if anybody knew he was himself and not other people, it was Oscar Wilde.

By way of contrast, Pissarro's *Woman Washing Dishes* is not a portrait: a wonderful painting, not unevocative of the woman's character, but not evocative enough of a lived life to be a portrait. There's not enough self being performed here. And, intriguingly, she has no name. Without a name, an image can't quite make the leap into a lived life. If Pissarro had called his painting *Marie Dupont Washing Dishes*, it might, with a squeak, have just passed muster.

Even so, this woman in a brown dress and white cap washing dishes in a laneway lacks what we mean by (and I have recourse to Brilliant's own phrase) 'an irreducible soul'. This word 'soul' must be forced out of hiding at this point. No other, except, barely, 'psyche', will quite do to describe this integrated, conscious self I think we agree to be tricked into seeing in a good portrait. Paul Bloom speaks of 'essences', George Steiner likes 'presences', but let's go with the simpler, old-fashioned 'soul' for the time being.

One attribute of a soul, which the finest portrait painters seem to capture and which chair legs, rosebushes, even skeletons – and, arguably, mere earthworms or streptococci – do not possess, is the ability to answer the question: what is it like to be you? Or at least, in the case of humans, dogs, cows, parrots and so on, down to about goldfish, it is not unreasonable to wonder what it's like to be them and to imagine they would have an answer if they could speak.

The considered answer to this question, it seems to me, would always involve an awareness of being not so much a moving thing, able to be arrested at a given point in time and space, as the movement itself, a kind of endless 'becoming' or changing connection with the world, experienced uniquely.

Just a complex brain function, some would say, an illusion, but it's a beguiling one. It begs to be believed in. And when I first saw colours appear on Robert Hannaford's portrait – the eyes, the skin on my face and hands – I knew I was being teased, I knew there was only one of me, not two, I knew there was no 'soul' imbuing the canvas, but all the same . . .

It's not necessarily a question of photographic likeness, this art of capturing the soul. In the famous portrait of Elizabeth I in the National Portrait Gallery, for instance (the Ditchley Portrait, as it's often called, commissioned by Sir Henry Lee), although the severely vacant face is taken from life and is recognisable as the queen's, there is no soul. Nor is there meant to be: this painted, wigged, bejewelled and sumptuously clad figure, pale as porcelain, anatomically freakish, is simply a coded message about English might and wealth and Sir Henry Lee's admiration for his sovereign.

Just over two decades after Sir Henry Lee commissioned his Ditchley Portrait, however, in 1616 or thereabouts, William Larkin painted a portrait of the king's favourite, George Villiers, the first Duke of Buckingham, Groom of the Bedchamber as well as future Marquess, Lord High Admiral and virtual king of England. This painting not only signals Buckingham's wealth and power (he's wearing the spectacular robes of a Knight of the Order of the Garter, drawn back to reveal his astonishing showgirl legs), and not only captures Buckingham's distinctive beauty (he was reputed to be the most handsome man in England, whatever that might mean) and his character (ruthless, inept, cloying, sexually opportunistic), but, for want of a better expression, his 'soul'.

There is psychic movement here, in other words, as there is not in the Ditchley Portrait of Elizabeth. There is a sense of a lived life caught lightly but with devastating skill. James I was besotted with his 'sweet boy' Buckingham – he loved him 'more than anyone else', he told the Privy Council a year after this portrait was painted – and in the provocative stance and the coy smile on his reddened lips the artist has instantly exposed a life lived out in coteries of male favourites eager to pander to the king's susceptibilities. There is movement forwards as well: this peacock is set to soar. And soar he did, as we know – so intolerably high that he had to be murdered when still quite young.

Standing in front of the Ditchley Portrait – a thin-faced, ageing figurine swathed in clouds of white silk laced with pearls and rubies – we do not smile. This is the imperial virgin, scarcely even a woman. But when I first set eyes on Buckingham, I not only smiled, but turned to find a companion to share my glee. The legs and the lips don't quite account for it. But what can?

Over the week or more I sat in that chair in Robert Hannaford's studio, my head tilted just so, my hands clasped just so in my lap, my left leg thrown over my right just so, I watched him take hold of my soul, minute by minute, hour by hour – yet I still can't say quite how he did it. One of the tricks is obvious: traditionally, the artist has surrounded the figure of the living subject with lifeless objects – in my case, a gluepot, a vase, a pencil, a couple of books, a mantelpiece and so on. Compared to them I am very much alive. Perhaps this is why modern painted portraits without these accoutrements – the Leo Schofield head, for example, by Brent Harris, or the Nick Cave – do not enchant us by inviting our connivance at a soul, however much we may admire or take pleasure in them as compositions, any more than Martin Sharp's Nimrod poster featuring Roy Rene's head does. Even John Brack's superb, completely unnaturalistic painting of Joan Croll, thanks to the carpet and chair, immediately invites us to consider what it might be like to be Joan Croll. She is alive in part because the carpet and chair are (so to speak) dead.

In some obvious sense Hannaford has caught a moment in his studio – a moment, it's true, held for perhaps ten days – but he's also caught something about my experience of being me in recent years: it's hard to find the precise words for it, but it's akin to a perplexed, yet peaceful, mindfulness. It's not exactly wistfulness – it's more active, more disabused, than that. It's a state imbued with the feelings you have when you've just said goodbye to somebody or something – watched a ship disappear over the horizon, for instance, with somebody you love on it. And there's a suggestion of hauteur as well.

At first I was a little taken aback by the figure's resignation, its slightly moony, unassertive quality – that's not how I think of myself, after all, remembering myself, as one does, as far more multicoloured – flirtatious at times, exuberant, playful, thrusting, annoyed, downcast, argumentative. But Hannaford was right, he knew his medium: it's dangerous to depict strong emotions in painted portraits – anger, surprise, delight, agitation – because they anchor the picture far too strongly in a given moment in a life, so that the illusion of the sweep of that life glimpsed through a particular moment disappears: the illusion that so strikes us in such celebrated portraits as Gerald Brockhurst's of Wallis, Duchess of Windsor or Thomas Phillips' of Lord Byron in the London gallery, or, here in Australia, Brett Whiteley's of Patrick White or Rupert Bunny's of Henry Handel Richardson. There are even some highly crafted photographic portraits where the photographer has conjured up this illusory appearance: Helmut Newton's portrait of Margaret Thatcher is a fine example. In Hannaford's portrait, the balance between the two illusions – the moment and the lived life – are, it seems to me now, almost perfect. To paraphrase John Berger on portraiture, he almost seems to be painting me, not so much waiting to have a relationship with him, as *having waited for this moment* to have a relationship with him, to be myself. As in all good portraits, he has caught both the moment *and* a sweep of time by catching me waiting to be seen by him.

During the sitting for the portrait, we hardly talked at all. I sat and he looked and, if he is to be believed, he painted what he saw. What he saw, though, whatever he might say to the contrary, must have been filtered through what he knew about my life from reading my books and listening to me over many years on the radio. To put it another way: he painted his living relationship with me.

This, by the way, does not mean, in any Wildean sense, that Hannaford 'painted himself'. The improbable idea that the painter actually paints himself has appealed to many writers on the subject of portraiture. Basil Hallwood, who paints the miraculous portrait of Dorian Gray, says that 'every portrait that is painted with feeling is a portrait of the artist, not the sitter. The sitter is merely the accident, the occasion.' That may have been true of the fictional Basil Hallwood, and it's a notion even Robert Hannaford has been quoted giving lip-service to – 'In the end,' he once told an interviewer, 'the portrait is as much of the artist as the sitter' – but I see no evidence of its being true of his portrait of me.

Wilde went further than his fictional hero. At another point in the novel, the suggestion is made that it is 'the spectator, and not life, that art really mirrors'. Then, in 'The Decay of Lying', he gives the spectator a serve as well: 'Most of our modern portrait painters are doomed to oblivion,' he writes. 'They never paint what they see. They paint what the public sees, and the public never sees anything.' Deliciously overstated, this last assertion contains the same grain of truth as the other two: a portrait reflects the painter's relationship with the sitter, which the spectator will interpret in the light of his or her own experience.

Hannaford recorded his relationship with me not only by creating my doppelgänger, and not only catching me waiting for him to see me. In this portrait in oils he plays subtle games with our (largely subconscious) expectations of portraits in oils.

Since the Renaissance, for example, as a visit to any European gallery makes plain, portraits in oils have traditionally, for the most part at least, depicted the virtuous – not in the banal sense of people who followed the Ten Commandments, never murdering anybody or committing adultery, but in the social sense of standing for what was considered admirable in a man or woman: a career at court or in the Church, good breeding, vast wealth, service to the state or empire. Hence all those duchesses and earls, all those admirals and lords and archbishops and men of property. They were dignitaries, not mere celebrities. In centuries nearer to our own, virtue embraced those who were acknowledged masters of their art – novelists, opera divas, even scientists: Adelina Patti, Sarah Bernhardt, Henry James, Virginia Woolf, Michael Faraday, Thomas Carlyle. (Nowadays, of course, virtue has been totally eclipsed by fame – anybody who has been on television will eventually be asked to sit for somebody.)

Now, I am neither a dignitary nor a celebrity. Although I have had my turn around the public arena, I do not embody what is usually considered admirable in Australian life (as David Campese, say, or, apparently, John Howard do, to name the subjects of two well-known portraits in the Canberra gallery.). My name is not a household word (as Kylie's or Germaine's is), my face does not stop the traffic (as Gough Whitlam's might, or Nick Cave's). And so my appearance in a portrait in oil in the National Portrait Gallery is, in a sense, an impertinence. And a mild impertinence is, of course, one of the qualities my writing and broadcasting career has been built around.

With status has generally come an air of invulnerability – although Thomas Cranmer, Archbishop of Canterbury, in Gerlach Flicke's famous portrait, strikes me as having some slight inkling of what was to come (he was to be burnt at the stake). As a rule, however, the barons and prime ministers, the kings and captains of industry lining the walls of the National Portrait Gallery ooze self-confidence. They're at ease with their power and their place in the sun. Part of our pleasure, I suspect, in examining these records of poised self-assurance lies in our knowledge that their stabs at immortality were, needless to say, all in vain – as ours will be.

Roland Barthes has suggested that all photographs, in contrast, are 'death masks', at least in the sense that the camera captures ephemerality, 'the death of the moment', in a way that the considered portrait in oils does not – indeed, as I am claiming, specifically avoids doing. Is this one of the reasons most of us feel uncomfortable about having our photograph taken? Does each candid snap resemble just a little too closely a record of our personal eggtimer, with only so many grains of sand left in the upper chamber? Both D. H. Lawrence and the poet Rilke hated photographs, I was reading recently, because they 'prefigured [the] end of becoming' – death, in other words.

Barthes' dictum is less true, I think, in the case of the carefully posed photographic portrait, the sort of photograph that does much more than just capture a moment, but, like the less banal portrait in oils, has sweep. This is what bewitches us, I think, in so many of Horst's portraits of the world's most famous people: they are untouched in his portraits, not just by our plebeian gaze, but by anything at all, let alone decay and death. This is what captivates us here in Canberra in Yann Gamblin's photograph of Elle Macpherson, Greg Barrett's of Maggie Tabberer or Andrew Rankin's of Ruth Cracknell.

Traditionally, however, portraits in oils hint at timeless virtue. In painting my hands and face as he did, Robert Hannaford not only undercut any pretension to immortality, but, in the very act of 'immortalising' the body and soul he saw before him on canvas, highlighted their vulnerability (although not weakness).

Perhaps in some Dutch portraits of seated male figures – unfleshly like me, just face and hands – there is a hint of perishability, but it's unusual in London or Canberra. 'You've made me look so . . . haggard,' I protested, while laughing, when he'd come to the end of his first full day's work on the face. (which brings to mind Picasso's quip when Gertrude Stein complained to him, 'But I don't look like that.' 'You will,' he said.) 'Haggard' was my (possibly ill-chosen) word for 'too precariously alive'. It was unexpected in a portrait. But it was spot-on: wasn't 'precariously alive' the very quality, after all, I had so recently made my name with in *Night Letters*?

Touché!

(And speaking of *touché*, sitting *is* a kind of duel, by the way: there is hardly a painted portrait in existence that shows no hint of the battle between painter and sitter that takes place daily in the studio. I resort to every ruse a frozen form is capable of to make sure I am represented as being who I know I am, while the painter silently, stroke by stroke, forces me to submit utterly to his grander and subtler design.)

On first seeing the portrait in the Archibald exhibition in Sydney, a critic in the *Sydney Morning Herald* remarked that the most interesting thing about the painting was my appalling taste in clothes. Even in modern portraits one expects a certain standard, a sense that the chosen attire will reflect, if not status (nowadays), then at least the appropriate milieu. Judges' robes, a football jersey, twinset and pearls, a grubby painter's smock, even no clothes at all – it doesn't matter what the subject is wearing, as long as the clothing – or in Germaine Greer's case, the lack of it – amplifies our sense of why it's appropriate for this painting of this particular figure to be hanging here at all.

Yet in Hannaford's portrait I appear to have turned up at his studio in a grab bag of garments picked up in haste from the bedroom floor: a lumpy blue sweater, crumpled jeans, plum-coloured socks and an old leather jacket, years too young for me, best kept, some might have thought, for walking the dog late at night in the backstreets of Fitzroy.

Now, for the record, I was cold. For hours on end, day after day, I had to sit stock-still in a poorly heated room in wintry Adelaide. So I rugged up. What happened then was that Robert Hannaford rather liked the way the shine on my leather jacket matched the shine on my shoes – not quite in the same league as the silken gleam on Elizabeth's dress or Buckingham's stockings, but we suspect a cheeky nod in that direction – and the red of the socks is alluded to in a red pencil, a striped cup and my unironed shirt. My dishevelled, almost gaudy appearance, against a background of *soigné* writers dressed to kill, suggests ordinariness. It is so unremarkable that it even fails to be op-shop chic. The ordinariness of this man in a chair in Hannaford's painting, accentuated by the glaring everydayness of his clothing, declares out loud: I have no fixed position in any cultural parade; I assume no set place in the pageant of national identity – despite the fact that, subsequently, the portrait was to hang in an institution that exists in part to create this very kind of pageant: the National Portrait Gallery in Canberra. More importantly, the ordinary, and how to redeem it, has been a constant theme, almost an obsession, in all my writing, especially in the novel *Corfu*.

As I see it, then, unwittingly or not, Hannaford has hoodwinked us into seeing a soul in his painting not just by what a writer friend of mine calls 'that tiny dab of white in the eye', but by playing a number of subtler games with our expectations of portraiture.

And just for a moment, I think, as their eyes come to rest on my double, most viewers will connive happily at the illusion.

∽

Part of the shock for me as sitter, watching my likeness take shape on the canvas to my left, came from the realisation that when I paint portraits – in sound, of course, not paint – and in particular anything resembling a self-portrait, the body is barely present. In fact, the more I write, the less a description of the body seems to count in creating the illusion of a self. In the novel *Corfu*, for instance, the narrator has no physical characteristics that set him apart from other human beings at all: he is neither fat nor thin, neither tall nor short, neither fair nor dark, neither handsome nor plain, and, although his age can be calculated by reference to external events, he is never referred to as either young or old. Indeed, he only seems to have a gender for architectonic reasons: his life turns out to be a shadow-play of another male character's. This nameless narrator is a lightly tinted, transparent space in the novel's fabric – yet I believe he has psychic substance. He exists as words, used in an individual way, describing thoughts and feelings.

So this lumpily clad, fleshly presence beside me is an affront.

Obviously my characters have all the basic bodily equipment – they run their fingers through their hair, blink and cast glances, stretch their legs out and elbow people aside – but it is not as a rule the configuration of their bodily parts that marks each of them out as a distinct subject. As I sat hour after hour, day after day, staring straight ahead in Robert Hannaford's chair, I had plenty of time to reflect on what we share, portrait painters and I as a writer, and what we approach very differently.

In a lecture she gave at the National Portrait Gallery in London in 2000, A. S. Byatt made it quite clear that, when it comes to portraits, she believes painters and writers have little in common. 'Portraits in words and portraits in paint are opposites,' she said at the beginning of her lecture, 'rather than metaphors for each other.' Her reasons for calling them 'opposites' seem to boil down to two: the first concerns the momentariness of a painting (in its execution and our engagement with it) as opposed to the time it takes to write or read a story; and the second concerns what paintings and stories can depict. I find her argument too sweeping. I think it's more a matter of a difference in the approach to representation than of opposites.

If we take, for example, the famous Whiteley portrait of Patrick White and compare it with David Marr's biography of the writer, then certainly, at some obvious level, the Whiteley picture can be said to be arrested in time: the viewer engages with a depiction of the writer at a particular point in his life (he was sixty-seven), in a particular room (the downstairs living room) of his house in Martin Road, while Marr's book homes in on a moving target over a lifetime. Yet, if we look more closely at the Whiteley, we notice immediately that Patrick White is not quite as motionless or arrested a figure as he appears to be: the impossible view through the doors to the Opera House and a parched Centennial Park make us wonder what those marvellously painted eyes are seeing, what they have known and lived through, while his desk is a veritable archive of a lifetime's loves (and hates, as it happens). There is movement here, but it's narrated centrifugally and with obvious artifice, rather than sequentially and 'realistically', as it is in Marr's biography.

Indeed, I would obviously take the argument further: what distinguishes a fine portrait from a banal snapshot, in my view, is precisely its lack of momentariness.

A painted portrait, Byatt then argues, can depict little more than visible surfaces, whereas a portrait in a story can not only depict 'invisible things' as well – thought processes, loves, antipathies, transformations – but leaves the reader free to construct 'endlessly varying visual images' of the bodies and clothing described. Again, at a superficial level, Byatt is right: over some seven hundred pages Marr can describe in abundant detail the 'invisible things' we can only guess at by looking at the Whiteley, but we *can* guess at some of them: White's view of himself as a 'monster', for example, his cantankerousness, his wit, his strength of character, his love for Manoly, perhaps even something about his aesthetics. I don't feel my imagination constrained, either, by Whiteley's rendition of White's body and clothing – directed, perhaps, but not limited. I can imagine other Whites.

Again, to take the argument a little further, I would suggest that painters can sometimes capture qualities a writer would have difficulty finding words for. Clearly I had difficulty finding quite the right words to describe the self Hannaford painted in his portrait of me.

On reflection, I think A. S. Byatt's assertion is grounded too simplistically in one kind of story-writing and one kind of portraiture. Surely it is less a matter of 'opposites' than of asking different things of the spectator's or reader's imagination. Sitting in Robert Hannaford's chair, ruminating on writing and painting, I had in mind autobiographical and fictional writing of my own and cast about for painters whose techniques I felt an affinity for.

My mind settled on pictures from an era I have always found resonates with something fundamental to my ideas of beauty and pleasure. It's more a matter of an era than a school: all the painters my mind flew to, with one exception, were born, roughly speaking, in the 1870s and early 1880s. The reason for this resonance is probably very simple: when I was a small boy, a neighbour who was an amateur artist took to giving me, on special occasions, small books of reproductions by famous artists. El Greco I found affecting, but repugnant, but once we got onto Cézanne, and then Picasso, something struck a strong chord – although which chord I could not have told you. I was, after all, only eight or nine years of age. Matisse and Modigliani had to wait until much later.

Of all the painters I got to know through these booklets (still on my shelves), however, the one who completely captivated me as a child was the man one Australian critic has dismissed as 'the French Ken Done': Raoul Dufy. What still appeals to me about Dufy (indeed about all the fauves) was the way life was not imitated but evoked in my mind by planes of strong colour forced into patterns, almost against their will, by black or dark-coloured lines, often drawn as if in haste, impressionistically. It was almost as if the real subject of some of these canvases was the very experience of rhythm and colour – as in Dufy's *Red Concert*, an explosion of deep red light – which he then scribbled over in order to observe the conventions. In other words, the Dufy paintings I loved, such as *The Bay of Sainte-Adresse* or *The Mediterranean*, were nothing more than brightly coloured, articulated spaces, vaguely evocative of real mornings or afternoons in real places, for which I could fill in the detail in my mind.

The jockey and top-hatted racegoers in *Race Track* and the conductor and musicians in *Red Concert* are little more than splodges of colour escaping black outlines. In fact, some of the racegoers strike you as nothing more than patches of green turf turned as an afterthought into cartoons of human figures: two arms, two legs, a torso and child's sketch of a human face, that's all. Yet I am at Ascot – or is it Longchamp? – on race day; I can almost smell the horse sweat and the sun on the grass; and although I don't know what they're playing at the red concert, I can hear Shostakovich loud and clear. Dufy makes me an artist. In a closely analogous way, when I write, it gives me pleasure to think I may be turning my readers into autobiographers and storytellers.

Dufy, of course, is not noted for his portraits. Turning my thoughts to well-known portraits by the artists I feel an affinity to, I can begin to see more clearly what it is we have in common when we 'paint'. In portraits such as Modigliani's of the Spanish painter Juan Gris, or of his mistress Jeanne Hébuterne (both seen in Australia in 1986 in the Twentieth Century Masters exhibition in Canberra and Brisbane), while one imagines that he has captured some resemblance to living people (Gris is clearly not a Viking but a dark-haired, dark-eyed young man with a strong jawline, Hébuterne not a Mexican peasant but a slender, auburn-haired woman with a long, oval face), the artist is painting more than a likeness: the Gris, with its recasting of the face and neck into separate planes is also about Gris' (and Modigliani's) cubist vision, as well, perhaps, as being about Modigliani's love of African carving, while the Hébuterne is about the rhythms of arcs, ovals and ellipses – and also, curiously, intimacy (it's all in the drooping smock and her curved form backed into a corner).

In other words, it is the rhythmic articulation of space that breathes life into these paintings, rather than any easy *aide-mémoire* likeness to living people.

Years – in fact, decades – of studying, and loving, Russian realists such as Tolstoy and Turgenev, with their unrelenting detailing of bodies, clothes, voices, laughter, gestures and gaits, has had remarkably little effect on my penchant for this post-impressionist technique (if that is the right word), heralded by Cézanne, for representing human subjects. Turgenev's description of Zinaida in *First Love*, for instance, is exhaustive and exhausting: in two short paragraphs I learn that Zinaida is 'a tall, slender girl in a striped pink dress with a white kerchief on her head . . . [and there is] something . . . enchanting, imperious and caressing, something mocking and charming' in her movements. The smitten narrator dwells in adolescent torment on her 'lovely fingers . . . the graceful figure, the lovely neck, the beautiful arms, the slightly dishevelled fair hair under the white kerchief – and the half-closed, perceptive eyes, the lashes, the soft cheek beneath them . . . the large grey eyes in a bright, lively face . . . the gleam of white teeth, the droll lift of the eyebrows'. (We learn even more a few lines further on: Zinaida's smile is 'mocking' and at the same time 'bright and sly', her 'caressing voice' sounds like 'silver', her look is 'swift and radiant', her hair 'soft and golden', her throat 'unblemished' – and on top of all that comes a description of what she was wearing!)

It's too much. Despite A. S. Byatt's vision of a reader freed to construct 'endlessly varying visual images' by a storyteller's portrait of a character, I, as Turgenev's reader, feel almost *de trop* here. I enjoy all the 'oh' and 'oo' sounds in the Russian – Turgenev's Russian is nothing if not euphonious – but I am just a voyeur: having read it twice, I want to read something else. I want to be more when I read: I want to be a writer as well; I want to take part in an act of creation.

On the other hand, when I look at Matisse's *Portrait of Madame Matisse. The Green Line* (1905) – a simple face-shaped patchwork of quite unlifelike greens, yellows, violets, blues and orange-reds – I feel drawn (perhaps mistakenly) into a whole world of anxious experience, muteness, self-absorption, domesticity and desire. The wonder lingers – as it does, for me, in what is perhaps my favourite Australian portrait: Sam Fullbrook's heartbreaking painting of Ernestine Hill.

Wonder is more of a problem for a writer than it is for a painter (or a poet or composer) – and for a reason directly related to Byatt's sense of a painted picture as embodying comparative momentariness. Wonder impales you suddenly on a shaft of beauty. Springing from a half-dark place beyond your understanding, it pierces you unexpectedly and incomprehensibly, like sorcery or a religious vision, leaving you half-bereaved, nostalgic for the instant you were first transfixed, while at the same time hankering for a reasonable explanation of what you've seen. Passages of music, paintings, lines of poetry, not to mention glimpses of flying saucers or the Virgin Mary, can stop time for us in this way, while novels, memoirs and discursive essays, tied as they are to reasoning and to unravelling time, must make do with the odd magician's trick (no sorcery here) or moment of pleasurable surprise. In other words, while I might seduce you into imagining a living self in your mind as you read, I cannot, as a writer, replicate that moment of wonder when you walk into or out of a room in a gallery and, just for a second or two, the twinkling of an eye, you feel the presence of a ghost – of sorcery, not some mere sleight of hand.

It is said that Dufy had a 'great eye for music' – and certainly a work such as his *Blue Mozart* paints the sound of a Mozart allegretto to perfection. My task as a writer is to refine my ear for rhythmic shape and colour, to make my outlines fool you into seeing them move and think and speak against a solid, plausible background like one of Matisse's rugs, and then to stand aside as you mistake my confection of sound for 'reality'. Nevertheless, however 'real' my characters, they will never coax you into conniving at their separate, self-conscious existence – you will always know the magic-lantern show is just rolling in your mind. If, on my better days, I am an adroit magician, any true sorcery, when you read my books, is your affair.

In a portrait gallery, however, I think something more primal haunts the rooms and corridors. Here, each time we turn a corner or glance around us at the actors, dukes or footballers hanging on the walls, we risk falling under a spell – just for an instant, just for the length of time it takes to remember that a rainbow is not a miracle. That's not simply a canvas smeared with paint – a head, two arms, a torso and two knees, we catch ourselves thinking in a burst of primitive perception. There's somebody actually caught in there!

But it's not the actor, duke or footballer who's been caught – it's us.

∼

I wonder sometimes if Dufy irreparably skewed my view of the world. It's embarrassing to have been so profoundly influenced by someone second-rate, but he seduced me when I was still so young and innocent. Like any youthful infatuation, though, it has shaped how I love. And think and write, naturally, but also actually love.

It's not just a matter of the 'articulated spaces' or the explosions of light that cast a spell on me. It's not just his palette of lilacs, mauves and heliotropes, or the way he gashes his cobalt bays and sapphire skies with indigo or white: it's the yellow towns themselves, the way they glow, the vibrant peopledness of everything – even his empty rooms seem to be resting from lives lived irrepressibly but gracefully. Serene as butterflies, these paintings are yet quivering. Violent, but in a childlike way. Sensual, rhythmic, refined – each canvas an allegretto. Not like Lane Cove at all. The only thing that quivered at our place was the Kelvinator.

In other words, it was the turquoise dream of somewhere else – that's what enchanted me. Somewhere Mediterranean – Nice, Naples, Sicily, but also, like his *Casino in Nice* (a golden fantasy with cupola and towers, floating beyond the palm trees in the foreground on a purplish sea), somewhere evocative of the Levant. (There, you see – there's my Sotadic zone taking shape already. And how old was I? Eight?) And once ravished, I never really recovered my innocence.

Now I think about it, it all comes together. What seized Dufy's painterly imagination, it turns out, and emboldened him to revel in his love of strong colours and daring brushstrokes was a single beach scene from 1904 by Matisse: *Luxe, Calme et Volupté*. (The Matisse doesn't bowl me over, now I look at it again. It's not quite sensuous enough – too many pinks and yellows.) Matisse in his turn was responding to Baudelaire's poem 'L'Invitation au voyage'. I hadn't read it since my student days, but I've just found it again in a copy of *Les Fleurs du mal* that has been jammed unloved on a bookshelf between Beckett and Camus for half a lifetime. Immediately everything falls into place: the dream of travel with a lover '*au-delà*' – 'into the beyond' (wherever that is – somewhere steamy and amber-coloured) where 'all is order and beauty, / Sumptuousness, calm and voluptuous pleasure'. The poem is saturated with 'Oriental splendours', a vagabond mood and the warm light of setting suns that clothe everything in hyacinth and gold. It is a polished musical performance in French, an exquisite evocation of inner landscapes, but it still strikes me this morning as rather lushly trite, to be honest. All shimmering surfaces with nothing underneath (well, that's symbolism for you), the sort of thing you should grow out of. I never quite did. Once you lose your virtue to Dufy and his teachers Matisse and Baudelaire, you apparently lose it for life.

Maybe that's one of the reasons I've never quite managed to love Australia. I'm sure it's one of the reasons that the first thing I can ever remember writing, on the back verandah of our house in Lane Cove, staring out at the forest of eucalypts creeping up out of the gully into our very backyard, was a story set in Istanbul (which I'd never seen), studded with turquoise tiles. And I remember using the phrase 'mindless sky' about the sky above my head in Lane Cove.

Australia is a likeable country (on the whole), and I do like living here – I have no abiding desire to live anywhere else – but it's not my dream (my fantasy being of some olive-skinned *au-delà*), and the reality of 'Australia', unlike the reality of Portugal, say, or Japan, is curiously hard to seize hold of – it's just too nebulous a concept. And the more nebulous it becomes, the more stridently it proclaims its existence. You can point to a shape on the map called 'Australia', but on closer inspection nothing coheres, it doesn't hang together, it lacks the sort of glue that makes Portugal Portugal and Japan Japan. Moreover, the second-rate quality of so much of our public life seems unredeemed by anything – history, ideals, cultural tradition, any of those things that might have provided a bit of glue. Dynamism isn't enough. It feels second-rate all the way down. To love your country in the way many Portuguese and Japanese do, your dreams and reality must at least overlap. You must feel you have at least some allegiance to what your country prides itself in. The country has to first of all exist. I don't feel the sort of hostility towards my native land that D. H. Lawrence claimed to feel towards England. 'I curse my country with my soul and body,' he wrote, 'it is a country accursed physically and spiritually. Let it be accursed forever, accursed and blasted. Let the seas swallow it …' I just lack any passion for it and hanker after more of what a francophile artist friend of mine calls *composition* – in the landscape, the architecture, the public culture. I feel wistful for a native land that is cosmopolitan rather than multicultural.

I can see a bit of Australia from my window and it's spectacularly beautiful. I love it – the huge blue mountain tumbling the houses at its foot into the river shimmering in the wind – but I don't think of it as 'Australia'. It's just where I live – and do my vagabond dreaming. 'Australia' still feels to me like someone else's dream. A few years back I wrote about Australia and dreams for the Italian journal *Nuovi argomenti*, trying to explain to Italians how I thought about these things.

Australia

Australia, in a sense, was dreamt up. It *had* to be there, according to the Greeks, to stop a top-heavy earth capsizing and tumbling head over heels into emptiness. Nearly two thousand years ago in Alexandria, Ptolemy imagined a vast, unknown land in the south, ribbed with mountain ranges, weighing down the earth, keeping it upright.

In ancient times Europeans were always dreaming fabulous dreams of the edges of the earth, as we know. For centuries they spun wondrous fictions about what lay beyond the Pillars of Hercules, beyond India, beyond the Black Sea, beyond Ethiopia. There snakes sprouted wings, trees grew ebony, stones smelt of frankincense and tasted of honey, fox-sized ants dug for gold, and men were freaks with one eye, no nostrils and ears that looped to the ground. But these fictions were always at some level playful, there was always some element in them of playing to the crowd – look how Herodotus or Strabo or Ctesias offer them to us, almost as an entertainment, a sort of ancient *X-Files*. In any case, the strands of knowledge linking the Mediterranean to India, China, Siberia, West Africa – even, in all probability, to Scandinavia – were real. The thinnest tracings sometimes, but real. People met people who'd met people who'd met people who'd been up the Volga, spun silk in China or sailed down the West African coast. Australia (as far as we know) was purely imagined.

It's true that Italian traders in India or Vietnam in Ptolemy's time may have heard rumours, or rumours of rumours, of a great land to the south, and loosed them in the streets of Rome when they got home, but there's no evidence for it, none at all. Obviously a junk or two may have been blown southwards off-course, obviously a wide-eyed fisherman may have spread tales in some market-place amongst the date palms of things he claimed he'd seen. Who knows what stories drifted on the spice-laden air where European traders gathered two thousand years ago? Nobody knows, nor can we know. As far as we *know*, until not so long ago, Australia just existed in people's heads. Not even the locals thought in terms of 'Australia'.

It also existed on maps – delicately coloured, lopsided, fantastical maps which are still a mystery. In the Middle Ages maps of the world showed a fourth continent with fabulous inhabitants – woolly griffons, for example, and men who shaded themselves from the torrid sun with their gigantic feet. Then, just over four hundred years ago, cartographers started drawing maps (in pinks and deep creams with a wash of green in places) that showed the outline of what proved to be there. Before anyone from outside ever came here (as far as we *know*), there it was, taking solid shape, with bays and promontories, rivers and mountains, south-east of Java. No longer a jagged lump at the bottom of the world, as Ptolemy had pictured it, the southern land had drifted rather abruptly north (as in geophysical terms it actually had), a little closer to hand, almost putting itself in the way of the Portuguese and Spanish seamen poking about in the Spice Isles to the north.

And then Dutchmen started to bump into it, of course, just where the French mapmakers had foreseen they would. Some say the Portuguese bumped into it first, but that's something we still can't be sure of. It hardly matters. What matters is that in the seventeenth century the coastline began to inch eastwards across the map in intricate detail into nothingness, a shrinking nothingness waiting for the English finally to fill it in almost two centuries later. Then *Terra australis incognita* was at last ready to become 'Australia'.

⁓

Are we then just the figment of some Europeans' imagination? Of course not – that's not my point at all. There's nothing ectoplasmic about the city I'm looking at outside my window as I write these lines. And when a local inhabitant speared to death a Dutchman from the *Duyfken* in 1606 during the first known European encounter with the south land, this hunter clearly didn't feel 'thought up' by anyone. Nor, I dare say, did the dying Dutchman feel pierced by a dream.

All the same, there's a tantalising sense in which, until these two men's worlds collided, they were unreal to each other. *And to some extent still are.*

In fact, it seems that the original inhabitants of this continent did not even dream of an 'outside' they had links to. Their diverse world-creation stories seem to be about 'here': about the activities of the ancestor spirits beneath and on the known landscape; about the sacramental nature of *this* land, with little curiosity about the existence of a 'somewhere else'. In English, rather confusingly, we use the word 'dreaming' to describe this creation time, as well as the stories about that time, the laws and symbolic systems growing out of these stories, some of them sacred and hidden, and the myriad ways in which the world is interpreted by different Aboriginal peoples. But actually the land was a real presence to these first inhabitants in a way the word 'dreaming' blurs.

Naturally, I can't know what the Dutchman's killer thought when he gazed at the horizon on the Gulf of Carpentaria. I know virtually nothing about the 'dreaming' of the people who lived around the Ducie River on Cape York in the early seventeenth century. Did he wonder what lay beyond the horizon? Did he wonder, for that matter, what on earth the horizon was? However, given what we do know about Aboriginal cosmogony in general, not to mention this man's likely experience of the world, it is improbable that he was curious about what lay beyond the horizon, at least in the way a Scythian warrior was, let alone Herodotus. I think that's a reasonable conclusion to draw.

When, for example, the fourteenth-century King of Mali set off for Mecca, he may not have been able to pinpoint where he lived on any map, nor would Henry the Navigator have had a clear idea a century later of how close his ships had sailed to the king's domains. Yet at least the King of Mali could set off across the Sahara for Cairo and Mecca along an established path, and there meet Muslims from India, China and even (for all I know) the Spice Islands. At least he was part of a grid – skewed and full of holes, but a grid nonetheless. Nowhere on this grid of knowledge, until recently, could you find Australia.

One day – no one knows for sure exactly when, but some years before the Dutchman was speared to death on Cape York in 1606 – a prau from Macassar, fishing for trepang, landed on the northern shore of the southern continent. I can still look at delicately detailed bark paintings of the praus that began to arrive from over the horizon every wet season, and at rock paintings as well – the rigging, the ropes, the upward-pointing bows, the squat Malay figures, they're all there. And during the wet season, the Malays built small settlements of houses on bamboo stilts, planted rice, smoked pipes, said Muslim prayers and flavoured the food in their pots with tamarind – the tamarind groves from the seeds they scattered are still there. The local Aborigines fished with them, helped them prepare the trepang in the huge metal boiling pots they brought with them, and even sailed back to Macassar with them for a look about. And the trepang found its way to China, popping up in Chinese medicinal treatises, and even poems, years before Captain Jansz made landfall on Cape York in the *Duyfken*.

Some say the Macassans were not the first Malays to bring knowledge of an outside world to Australia: there are song cycles about white rice boiling in pots made from the clay of anthills by a mysterious people called the Baiini long, long before the Macassans arrived. Whole families came, apparently, including women who wove cloth on looms, patterned with strange red, white and ochre triangles you can still see on wooden figures in Arnhem Land today. Some even say the Baiini came in the creation time and met the Great Ancestors, Djan'kawu and Laindjung.

Dutch or Portuguese, Macassans or Baiini, or Zanzibari Arabs, or Chinese . . . Who knows exactly when the two realities collided? What we *can* say is that several hundred years ago two grids of knowledge at last touched, giving coordinates for the land we came to call Australia.

Obviously there was something here all along – a network of established cultures, if not civilisations in the European sense of that word – but you can see how easy it is for someone living in this landscape even today to feel dreamt up, to want to tell the story of Australia's appearing in the ocean and on the maps as a kind of fulfilment of someone else's dream – the Ancestor Spirits', the Baiini's, Ptolemy's, the Dutch adventurers', it hardly matters whose.

The dream still hasn't quite become real. Somehow we still seem to be not fully awake. It's morning, but we're still drowsily trying to fit the landscapes of the night to what our eyes are telling us.

Somehow, even though I've studied maps of Australia breaking off from Antarctica fifty-three million years ago and drifting north; even though I've walked amongst banksias, prodded echidnas and watched mobs of kangaroos flit through the bush; even though I know two thousand generations of men and women have lived and died here, leaving traces we can carbon-date; even though I know the land has been surveyed and photographed from satellites thousands of times; and even though it says in my passport that I'm an Australian citizen, still I have difficulty believing that something called 'Australia' really exists.

My first dreams, as it happens, were of a 'beyond', an 'over there' almost as fantastical as early European dreams of us. I didn't really think I was here, you see, or only in the way you might wander backstage in a theatre by mistake and find yourself lost amongst stage props for the wrong play.

Snow was my obsession when I was very small. It's telling. Not cricket or model trains or tales of bushrangers or intrepid explorers, but snow. On Sydney's lower north shore, amongst the humid gullies choked with eucalyptus and lush native vines – and neat European gardens, as well: roses, sweet pea, geraniums, daisies – I would sit with books from the local library about glaciers, blizzards and snowdrifts, gazing at pictures of igloos and frozen lakes. Iceland and Greenland were almost enchanted domains to me, just as longed-for and phantasmagorical as *Terra australis* had once been for European mariners. One day, I remember, I heard that a neighbour's son had just come back from Iceland. I went and knocked on his door and looked at him as if he'd been to the Garden of Eden itself. He must have seen snow! His fingers must have reached out and touched snow! He must know the feeling of snow! Was it soft and smooth like ice-cream? Light? Frosty? How deep was the snow in Iceland? Did it pile up to the eaves?

What Freud might say about such an obsession, I can only dimly imagine. All I know is that snow meant 'over there', somewhere much more real than where I was. Snow lay on turrets and domes in London, for example, the most solidly real of any city on earth; it dusted famous Parisian squares and avenues; it lay in great drifts around the prison camps in Germany, from which my wartime heroes had escaped; it carpeted (in a word) the valleys and mountains where History had happened. Napoleon staggered home from Moscow through snow, the Dalai Lama looked out on snow from his window high in the Potala Palace; the West Was Won against a thrilling backdrop of snowy sierras on the screen at the local cinema.

When I did eventually see snow for the first time as a teenager in the Australian highlands – ragged pools of it amongst the granite boulders, mauvish sheets of it on shaded screes, forlorn, quite lifeless, hopelessly wet – I was disappointed. I'd expected something more . . . What? I couldn't have told you.

Forty or fifty years ago, I think almost all my dreams were in fact of elsewhere (Europe and America) and a former time. Apart from anything else, where I found myself (Sydney) lacked what I can only call *glamour*. It was *glamour* we didn't see about us in our comfortable streets of bungalows and gardens, and so we dreamt of it, especially when we were young. Or, at least, I think I did. It's a difficult English word to translate. What is it?

To be glamorous you have to be *à la mode* with people who matter – that goes without saying. (No one 'mattered' here in quite the way they did 'over there'. They still don't.) And physical beauty is a plus, of course, as is wealth, because they both evoke admiration, both bespeak power. But fashion, beauty, wealth and significance aren't the most important things: to be glamorous you must be part of a *pageant* of some sort, you must parade with others of your kind, decked out in all your expensive finery, to the applause of the crowd. Your significance lies in the crowd's applause, not in what you say or do. Yet our crowds were so small, their tastes so provincial, that their applause was hardly worth courting. Here no one important was watching. Life (in a depressingly post-colonial sense) was eventless.

To this day glamour very largely has its source overseas, where important things *happen*. We have pzazz aplenty – festivals, circuses, fireworks, blockbuster exhibitions – but little with deep roots *here*. To receive applause you still hear people peppering their conversation with references to some pageant they took part in elsewhere – in London, at Harvard University, on French television, anywhere but here. Only in the arena of sport do we believe in the worth of our own pageants. The Sydney Olympics – our very own enactment of a pageant from 'over there' – was about as dazzlingly glamorous as we could imagine anything being.

Unsporting by nature, I invented my own pageant to take part in. When I was still very small, I invented a land I could live in for some hours a day. It was neither in the historical past nor some science-fiction future, but in a different kind of mental space altogether, like a parallel universe. Sitting on the back verandah of our house (we spent half our lives on the back verandah), looking out at the green of our backyard – the lawn, the thickly wooded gully behind the house, always empty to the eye, but full of sounds – I began to create another kingdom in my head, an island kingdom *in the north* (naturally), where I could make things happen, significant things; where I could create a history, with kings and battles and revolutions; where the cities were beautiful, the snow-capped mountains spectacularly high, and everything was layered with the meaning I gave it. I even created a complex, highly expressive language for this realm, a language which has grown over the decades and which I still speak (although only to myself). I could describe to you the magazines in the railway kiosk in the capital city, the ferry timetable up the river, the menu in a certain café in a mountain resort I go to frequently, or the flowers in one of the botanical gardens. And the history of my land is rich as well: a layering of civilisations, migrations, hierarchies and rituals, recent battles between a totalitarian paradise and a liberal democracy – high drama wherever you look, from the Bronze Age to last week. Unlike where I live.

Perhaps what I've been trying to invent is a sense of history. Any child who is alone for much of the time (especially on warm afternoons after school, amongst quiet, green streets meandering between fingers of bushland) must be aware of being at the point where a voluminous past is threaded miraculously through the eye of the present moment, where vast folds of story and fable are squeezed into a microscopic point and fed into that instant that is you. But that's just a past, it isn't *history*. And so I dreamt my own solipsistic dreams of a history that made me real. I suppose my dreamt-up land will continue its vivid existence in my head until Australia itself becomes real.

In the meantime, I think I live in the antipodes rather than in something called Australia. The antipodes, after all, define themselves in terms of what they're on the opposite side of the globe *from*. The antipodean dreamer pinpoints himself on a mental, rather than physical map, his identity is a relationship to Europe (however oppositional), rather than an existence in a place. He keeps defining himself in terms of someone else's expectations of what is normal.

Some decades ago it began to look as if Australia might exist after all. It was an *intervallum lucidum* and did not last. For a short while the imaginative arts were encouraged, a base was laid for a home-grown intellectual culture, a clear-eyed gaze was cast on the history – indeed, the histories – of this continent (I had not even been taught Australian history at school), a sense of an Australian literary tradition began to form, of an Australian cinema . . . and it almost became possible to dream. We almost became a sovereign people. But it had all come too late.

One of the striking things about Australia now is the burying of history under a multiplicity of pasts. In this 'new country', everything seems paradoxically so old. Each migrant community energetically embalms its past – indeed, is officially encouraged to embalm and revere it – to the point where the landscape is now littered with the corpses of traditions long buried in the home countries. Hundreds of heritages are transported to this 'new country', unpacked and lovingly set up like sacred shrines, tended by worshippers who seem largely oblivious of where they are now. Where they are now is a blank space. In a postmodern frenzy we celebrate the diversity, the profusion of pasts – Chinese dragons at Chinese New Year, traditional Thai curries, Estonian folk-singing festivals, Hmong weaving, British colonial architecture, Tibetan religious rituals, Aboriginal bark painting . . . It's very colourful, it's an interactive museum, but what we still don't have is a sense of a shared history, of a real now.

And without a sense of a shared history (even if it's skewed or unreliable) I think it's hard to dream anything but highly solipsistic, if colourful, dreams. To a large extent we're still stuck dreaming other people's dreams of who – and where – we are.

There's another problem for the Australian dreamer at the turn of the century, too: globalisation. As a distant province of the great Empire ruled from 'over there', our imaginations are increasingly swamped with other people's cultural images. I have only to talk with my neighbours in our street to be struck with how rigidly defined our dreams are by cultures which have no connection with our land. Can we imagine friendship any more, for instance, without memories of *Friends, Seinfeld* and *The Simpsons*? Can we imagine gardens without memories of traditional English gardens or even traditional Japanese gardens? Can we imagine policing society without thinking of *NYPD Blues* or *The Bill*? Hats, food, democracy, houses, religion, humour, even homosexuality – they're all difficult to imagine now without someone else's ideas about them flashing into our minds. Again, the postmodernists are in a frenzy of excitement about the vast smorgasbord of possibilities now on display on our computer and television screens, the vast hypermarket of images we can choose from, the huge switchboard in the sky we can all plug into, instantaneously communicating with Greenland, Rome, Macassar, Tokyo, Mali . . .

It *is* exciting. But it makes an Australian dreaming almost impossible. It leaves us still consuming other people's dreams about what it might mean to be us.

⌒

When at the end of the last millennium the majority of Australians voted to remain subjects of the English Queen, the true tragedy, I think, was not in our failure to reinvent ourselves as a republic – to all intents and purposes we are already a republic – the tragedy lay in our declaration to the world that we still only exist as part of someone else's past, that we still have no strong sense of a distinct, eventful, historical reality, that our meaning in the world is still a borrowed one.

Of course, we never were a particularly imaginative people. Our strength has always lain in our pragmatism, our ability to do things, in our mimetic arts. During that *intervallum lucidum* I mentioned, a different kind of strength seemed about to be born, but fear, and foreign intervention, soon put us back in our box. Now, at the beginning of the new millennium, ignorant of our history and cynical about our independence, I don't think many of us are bothering to dream of anything except surviving as comfortably as possible.

Is there any glimmer of hope for the dreamer? Perhaps a small one. Very slowly, almost imperceptibly, there's a consciousness growing that there is one thing we all do share, something with a history (not just a past), something that is not dreamt up but is actually there, something with an incredibly rich life of its own (if only you have the eyes to see), something unlike anything Hollywood or *Seinfeld* or the Pope or the Queen of England or the president of Mitsubishi could ever conceive of: the land. We thought it might be the Garden of Eden, we thought we might turn it into another England, we thought it could perhaps be converted into real estate – but we were wrong. When it becomes real to us, and we belong to it (rather than it to us), then we might be able to start dreaming again – kaleidoscopically, swoopingly, with gentle fruitfulness. Then there will be such a place as Australia.

⁓

Meanwhile, I find it hard to love with a passion this place my passport says I'm a citizen of. I hope this doesn't sound sour – I don't feel sour, just unmoved. Perhaps love will indeed flower one day, as it's said to do in other kinds of arranged marriages, but it's taking its time. Ever since I was about eight, when Mr Bennett at Lane Cove Primary School asked me in front of the whole sniggering class if I was 'foreign', I've been aware of being a ring-in on the team – Team Australia. It wasn't an openly hostile question, but it served as an early warning to watch my step in public as the odd man out. There are safety zones all over the country where those of us out of step with 'Australia' can find refuge amongst kindred souls and breathe easy (radio stations we can listen to, bookshops where we can find sustenance, cafés, art galleries and concert halls where we're welcome – the 'alternative universe' of latte-drinking, tertiary-educated, left-leaning frequenters of arthouse cinemas, pilloried with unrelenting vigour in the *Australian* newspaper), and I've tended not to wander too far from them. I've never been a fighter.

Perhaps that's at least partly why I shy away from sport. What is sport if not a parody of war (as exercising in a gym, for example, is a parody of labour)? Yet every Australian male is forced from early childhood to take this parody seriously. Given our addiction to war, it's hardly surprising. Ever true to the Anzac spirit, we tirelessly celebrate past military defeats and regularly offer up new batches of young Australians for slaughter in other people's wars, not having any of our own to fight. But it's not enough: the hunger to do battle remains unquenched. And so we fall back on make-believe wars. Needless to say, that's not enough either – 'massacring' Argentina, 'annihilating' Germany, 'thrashing' the French, all those 'victories', all those 'defeats' can never compete with real warfare – but it staves off the hunger.

And it goes further: as once he might have regarded military prowess as the very measure of his manliness, the young Australian male now looks to his sporting prowess for that measure. (Which is why women's netball is never going to seize the public imagination in quite the same way as football and cricket: at root, sport is about *male* virtues. On the front lines it's strictly men's business.) After school, several days a week, on the oval across the road from our first house in Hobart, for instance, grown men, barking obscenities, train up young boys to commit acts of violence against their adversaries in order to make them manly – and more: to make them securely Australian. One of our prime ministers, I now recall, actually called a cricketer the greatest Australian who had ever lived. And on the day she moved into her prime ministerial office, Australia's first woman prime minister ostentatiously plomped a football down in front of the Streeton landscape hanging over the mantelpiece. We got the message.

Now, I have no objection to people playing sport. There is something infantile about our obsession with it, from my point of view, and especially about our loyalty to clubs, resplendent of loyalty to schoolyard gangs, but for the most part I am simply indifferent to it, as I am to the royal family, say, Esperanto or children, which also have their champions. Consequently I am resentful at finding it squatting on more and more of the public arena, turning everything from TV comedy shows to parliamentary Question Time into a match. What I object to is the pretence that the hysteria over sport has anything to do with playing the game: it has been whipped up over the past few decades – basically since we have been able to watch sporting events live via satellite across the globe – in order to make media owners in the new worldwide market very rich. And it only works when there is a particular balance between highly developed skills and random disaster, as in gambling – that is to say, for football, golf, cricket and horse-racing, but not for athletics or archery. Nobody gets hysterical over archery competitions, except in Mongolia, and without hysteria nobody gets rich. And nobody gets either hysterical or rich from sport at a local level, which is why local sports clubs are in decline. It's not about sport, it's about money.

All the same, some people genuinely find sport aesthetically exhilarating, apparently, every bit as artistically satisfying as a night at Sadler's Wells. Who am I to argue? If they find two mobs of half-naked men grappling for a ball balletic, so be it. After all, in its own way, even football is transformative, as all great art is: it transforms battle into play. There's even a faint echo of chivalry there sometimes, as there no longer is in war.

Others, a little more ominously, thrill to the tribalism of sport. But, again, who can blame them? A bit of coherence in an increasingly atomised world – what could be more appealing? There's no better antidote to Weltschmerz, which seems to be all-pervasive at the moment, than a bit of tribal ra-ra-ra. As the Roman Empire fell apart a millennium and a half ago, my *Portable Gibbon* reminds me, Rome's 'idle multitudes' found succour in precisely this sort of spectacle for exactly the same reason. As in Australia today, the more frightening the emptiness at the centre became, the more frenziedly they flocked to mass entertainments. By the early fifth century AD, Gibbon tells us, the city's plebeians

> still considered the Circus as their home, their temple, and the seat of the republic. The impatient crowd rushed at the dawn of day to secure their places, and there were many who passed a sleepless and anxious night in the adjacent porticoes. From the morning to the evening, careless of the sun or of the rain, the spectators, who sometimes amounted to the number of four hundred thousand, remained in eager attention, their eyes fixed on the horses and charioteers, their minds agitated with hope and fear for the success of the colours which they espoused; and the happiness of Rome appeared to hang on the event of a race.

Sport, like war and shopping, offers hope. (Few commit suicide during war; nobody goes shopping, at least for whitegoods, when they are about to die.) Hope of what? Of victory, obviously, but also of consequence, even meaning. Who could object to that? After all, for most of us, ordinary life is little more than a succession of small humiliations, like a short story by William Trevor. Hope of moral uplift, too, at some level, with its roots in the murk of Victorian England – *mens sana* and all that. But, above all, sport, in the era of television and the internet, offers hope of heroism – or, more precisely, worldwide celebrity on a scale undreamt-of by Hollywood. And fabulous riches. Even sainthood. Johnny Depp and Tom Cruise are glamorous. David Beckham and Cristiano Ronaldo are gods.

Actually, as it happens, there's a new god in the firmament as I write: Andrés Iniesta, who kicked the deciding goal for Spain in the 2010 World Cup Final. As the entire universe is aware, he dedicated his winning goal to his close friend Dani Jarque by flashing his t-shirt inscribed: DANI JARQUE SIEMPRE CON NOSOTROS. (Jarque died suddenly at the age of twenty-four.) The BBC commentator, discussing this gesture with a Spanish sportswriter, was happy to use the word 'friend' over and over again, as in his turn was the Spaniard. In back-announcing the item, though, the ABC announcer couldn't bring himself to use the word 'friend'. 'Mate' would hardly do for a Spaniard, so he resorted to 'colleague'. Anything but 'friend'.

And that's another reason I find it hard to love 'Australia': the fear of friendship here. In the local paper the other week I was startled to see a picture of two Tasmanian men hugging – and apparently having a whale of a time doing it. Now, Frenchmen might hug, being Continental and secure in adult feelings of *fraternité*, as might footballers (*on the field*), but 'blokes' in Tasmania (to use the preferred term in the article accompanying the photograph) do not. To hug and stay 'blokey', it transpires, if you can't settle for a firm handshake, it's vital to do two things: maintain an A-frame stance (so that no dangly bits brush up against each other, presumably) and finish with a manly pat on the back.

But it is the article itself I find dispiriting. It's all about 'mates'. 'Friends' are at no point mentioned. The American equivalent of 'mate', 'buddy', also gets an airing. 'I've never given a second thought to hugging my mates,' says one of the huggers, a Burnie alderman. Has he had second thoughts about hugging his friends? Should he have had? Certainly, in England about three hundred years ago, men began to have second thoughts about hugging and switched to shaking hands. They did so, according to the historian Keith Thomas, because they'd finally dropped to the fact that some men had sexual feelings for their equals. While they restricted themselves to lusting after stable-boys or shepherds, nobody was particularly fussed – it was pretty much on a par with romping with the milkmaid, and hugging your friends was merely a sign of affection. But once it became clear that some men felt sexual desire for other men of their class, shaking hands seemed the safer option. It still is. So are 'mates', for much the same reason. Who knows what grown-up intimacies a word like 'friend' might encompass?

A few years ago, while listening to 3LO in Melbourne, I heard the then state premier refer to another member of his party as 'a friend and a mate of mine'. As he said it, I realised that he was making a distinction vital to the fabric of Australian society. When asked if another Labor backbencher was 'a mate', the premier said he was 'a friend'. Most listeners no doubt kept right on vacuuming the carpet or washing the car, imagining that the distinction Steve Bracks had made was of minimal importance. I, on the other hand, pricked up my ears, and shortly afterwards wrote a brief piece for the now defunct *Bulletin* magazine explaining why.

So Long, Mate

As the brouhaha over John Howard's desire to write 'mateship' into the Constitution showed, something about the idea is on the nose in postmodern, multicultural Australia. Many feminists, both female and male, are hostile to 'mateship'. To Eva Cox, for example, one of the country's best-known feminists, it smells of 'spew in the pubs . . . the gang-bang . . . testosterone poisoning'; Dale Spender calls it 'an inarticulate form of identifying and protecting your own and excluding others'; Barry Jones finds it 'archaic', a tradition harking back to the days when males bonded in adversity to 'fell trees, dig mines and fight wars'.

To ardent multiculturalists, mateship smacks of something they would probably call 'Anglo-Celtic'. They mean 'Irish', but 'Anglo-Celtic', referring as it does to a non-existent cultural tradition, is a usefully non-specific insult. In fact, many migrants are particularly enthusiastic users of 'mate' in the civil sense of the word ('Thanks, mate', 'Got a light, mate?' and so on). Here 'mate' means:

'For the purposes of this transaction, let's pretend we're equal and unarmed.'

On the whole, however, the feminists and multiculturalists are surely onto something. In a society where women have for decades been removing the barbed-wire fence around ideas about femininity (a few old machine-gun emplacements are still manned, of course), men by and large are still locked in competition for power with other males. Millions still spend their lives semaphoring messages to rival males about their superior ability to penetrate, procreate and protect their gene pools. Clothes, gait, accent, job descriptions, conversations about objects (cars, rising damp) and jousting rituals (such as football and office politics) are all signals in this exchange.

It's exhausting, dangerous work. One slip – a throwaway line about loving Gwen Harwood's poetry, for instance – and you're dead. In these circumstances, a man needs a safe haven, a trucial zone, where other males will not always be on the lookout for a chance to skewer you. The price of peace seems reasonable: total conformity to their expectations. These companions in conformity are 'mates'. They're your team. You bond with them against someone or something else – women, of course, but also Collingwood, the guys in management, bushfires, illegal immigrants, poofters, intellectuals, Liberal voters, Labor voters, parents, the young . . . It depends on where you see the threat coming from.

One of the myths about mateship, with a possible origin in the trenches, is that a mate will do anything for you. Over and over again in the interviews in Graham Little's book *Friendship*, men claim with considerable feeling that they would do 'anything' for a mate – the bond is so sacred that no call on it would be too great. And you would never dob in a mate, they all agree, with a kind of Sicilian solemnity, as if articulating a supreme moral virtue. In reality, of course, mates dob each other in all the time, starting in primary school, and it's just as well they do – Sicily is no one's idea of a civil society. And while they might help you move house once or, at a stretch, twice, they won't help three times and they certainly won't do your ironing for you.

So, if you think you're living in a war zone, mateship makes sense. If you don't, and don't see other men as rivals, friendship might strike you as a more appealing and enriching option.

Friendship is quite different from mateship and several generations of Australian men have not been good at it. It makes men who feel threatened by other males uncomfortable for several reasons. Apart from anything else, friendship, which implies emotional involvement with another and continual self-disclosure, can look suspiciously like coupledom with an unsettling erotic subtext. Consequently, many men feel happier dubbing their wife or lover their 'best friend'. (This is actually to miss the point: 'erotic' is not the same as 'sexual' and no sexual partnership is ever truly equal, as close friends are. As psychologists would say, sexual partners are complementary, whereas friends are symmetrically matched. Which is why you can never 'have a friend in Jesus'.)

The intimacy, exchange of vulnerabilities and mutual understanding between true friends is not cultivated *against* anyone, either. It's enjoyed, indeed craved, for what it is. It's freely chosen, too, unlike mateship. And it strengthens and affirms you not as a male, but as a human being. Women are often very good at it, and homosexuals usually have to be.

In different societies, naturally enough, friendship is expressed differently. In Mali, for instance, friends throw dung at each other and make rude remarks about each other's parents' genitals. In certain Mediterranean countries, friends are expected to observe reciprocity – I get you a good deal at Spiro's car yard, you introduce me to your sister's unattached friend – it's all in Homer, it's an ancient tradition. In Australia the shape of friendship is still in flux, but there are signs that some younger people are finding approaches to friendship and intimacy that their fathers and grandfathers, stuck in their wife plus mates scenario, would consider unmanly and suspicious.

All the same, in the kind of capitalist society we inhabit, with its emphasis on competition, work, productivity and the fun-house mirror world of sport, friendship is still difficult for men to enter into with any passion. Love – and friendship is one kind of love – remains disruptive if exercised outside the home. As a result, our emotional and psychological fabric is looking distinctly threadbare. The warp of male friendship is weak and sparse, the weft of mateship moth-eaten and brittle.

In a civilised society in the twenty-first century, I hope men will feel freer to leave signalling their prowess to the magpies and kangaroos. I hope more of us might consider bonding with other men and women in ways that pull down the barriers between individuals, leaving team jousting where it belongs – in the Middle Ages.

◡

What I failed to foresee when I wrote those lines was the arrival on the scene of a whole 'fun-house mirror world' of friendship on social networking sites on the internet. While the word has come back into vogue, its meaning has been cheapened to the point of utter triviality. The 'barriers between individuals' have certainly crumbled, but intimacy, the very heartbeat of friendship, is now just a rumour of what once was possible. Promising to connect us in clusters of friends in animated conversation with each other across the globe, the technology has instead turned us into a vast flock of narcissists, squawking into the aether about the trivia of our daily lives like flocks of bored seagulls scavenging for chips. Through overuse, the very word 'friend' now sounds trite.

It's not alone. The other day I was reading a long article about the Viennese writer Hugo von Hofmannsthal, whom I shall probably never get round to reading (which is why I was reading the article – one reads serious literary reviews in order not to have to read the books). One of Hofmannsthal's characters, Lord Philip Chandos, complains of losing his grasp on the language word by word: 'spirit', 'soul', 'body' – these words began to 'crumble in [his] mouth like rotting mushrooms'. Hofmannsthal was suffering from a touch of early modernism, apparently, although he never completely succumbed to it in the sense that Beckett or Joyce did.

I am immune to modernism, but I do know what he means by words that have rotted. 'God', for instance, turned to dust for me years ago – the word, that is – and I'm with Chandos entirely about 'spirit' and 'soul': like him I turn from these words with distrust bordering on distaste. (Transcendence is another matter entirely.) 'Community' is looking pretty mouldy to me, too, I have to say, along with 'democracy', 'family' and a number of other abstractions, including 'Australia'. (Perhaps it's indeed the word I feel alienated from, rather than the country.) For a while words such as these seem to conjure something up, and then one day, as they begin to wear through, you realise that there's nothing at all behind them. They've lost their point. What will be next? Will there be any words left?

'Homeland', however, still has a point for me. Zadie Smith mocks it deliciously in *White Teeth*, along with almost everything else we hold dear, calling it a 'magical fantasy word' like 'unicorn', 'soul' and 'infinity', but I still feel rather attached to it. Whatever my reservations about 'Australia', I do feel I have a homeland, although it's not a shape on a map and it doesn't issue passports: it's the English language. That's where I *belong*, that's what makes me feel stirrings of passion. And it's so wonderfully transportable: you can be safely at home in it anywhere from the Shetlands to Mumbai or the South Island of New Zealand. Even in America there are still enclaves where you can warm yourself at its hearth. I love to visit Russian and French, but my *patrie* is English.

Who knows where this kind of passion comes from? I can't help thinking that I may owe it to my adoptive father, Tom Jones, who, despite a rudimentary education in the 1890s at the hands of country-town nuns, sailed the world in the merchant navy when he was young, picking up bits and pieces of Cantonese, Malay, some Polynesian dialect or other and even a bit of Pashto from the Afghan camel drivers he hung around with in Port Augusta as a boy. *Satu, dua, tiga* he used to say sometimes, just for fun, when he was counting, or he might greet the dog in florid Pashto. And these smatterings of foreign languages meant that he fell in love with his own, flirting with English, playing with it, mocking it, bending it, making it jump through hoops as he bent it to his will. French, on the other hand, he treated with great respect, as it's usually wisest to do, as well as with a kind of wonderment. He played French by the rules. Tom didn't read books, he never quite saw the point of books, preferring life, but he delighted in language.

Or perhaps my passion for English comes simply from growing up in an era when people like us – lower middle class but with inner resources – listened to the ABC every night on the radio and when at the ABC speaking well was not a sign of elitism but of self-possession. In our family, whatever else we were (and nobody could have accused us of being 'normal'), we were always self-possessed.

I wonder if, having spent my entire childhood glued to an ABC where people spoke good English with pleasure, even on the children's programs, I was almost destined to spend a good slice of my senior years reflecting on language in some form or other on the ABC. Few were listening, I know that, but by the same token there was a scattering of eccentric listeners across the country who apparently liked to tune in to my meditations on literature and language. Just be yourself, I told myself, and let whoever wants to eavesdrop on your little disquisition on George Steiner, say, or the Nigerian novel, or translating from Russian, or euphemisms or Aboriginal languages, do so. On one occasion, not so long ago, I even spent fifteen minutes on the national airwaves holding forth on the arcane subject of the subjunctive. To my astonishment, it struck one of the strongest chords with my listeners that I could remember striking. A whole lot of people, it seemed, sensed that verbs are subject to some sort of mood change they can't quite get the hang of, and welcomed some clarification. They knew that there must be more to it than occasionally coming out with 'If I were you.'

I love the subjunctive. I've had a tremulously fond relationship with it ever since I first realised it was there. In fact, I find it quite difficult to feel warmly towards any language that doesn't have it. It pleads and cajoles, yet at the same time is shot through with self-doubt. It hasn't been well of late, it's true, in English-speaking countries, but it's far from dead. When given the chance on Radio National's *Lingua Franca* program, I offered it what I could in the way of support. I began with a sentence almost every Australian is familiar with.

The Subjunctive

'It's important to us,' the voice announces with mock sincerity hundreds of times a day all over the country, 'that you are aware of the safety features on board this aircraft.' Like all the other pedants on board, I flinch every time I hear it. What on earth can it mean? One thing it can't mean, obviously, is that it's important that we are aware of the safety features on board the aircraft for the simple reason that, for the most part, as the crew knows perfectly well, we're not. Unconvinced that any amount of pulling on cords or blowing on whistles will save us if the plane hits the water, we sit back, read our in-flight magazines and newspapers and wonder if by any chance we left the iron on.

No, what the voice must mean, surely, is that it is important that we *be* aware of the safety features aboard the aircraft. 'Excuse me! Hullo! Subjunctive!' I want to call out. 'It's not dead yet, you know! Why not use it for once, when it really matters?' But I don't, of course. I'd probably be frogmarched off the plane if

I did. And indeed (let's be frank): does it really matter? After all, I've worked out what the crew meant to say, haven't I, subjunctive or no subjunctive, and surely that's all that counts, isn't it? What they meant, even though it's not quite what they said, was: we want your compliance.

The point is that compliance is precisely what the subjunctive is there to encourage. This is the area it works in with most vigour. It has other delicate little tasks to perform as well, it's true, but it's on suggestion, stipulation, every gradation of requirement, preference, decree, request and enjoiner that the subjunctive thrives.

People's eyes tend to glaze over when you mention the subjunctive, in my experience. Some probably had a bad experience with it in French classes in childhood and still recall their horror the day it was revealed to them that learning all those nightmarish verb endings had just been the beginning: all French verbs, it transpired, had another darker, rather more spiteful side and it was called 'the subjunctive', which sounded like a disease and, like other people's religions, seemed complex, unfathomable and ultimately pointless.

Others – if they've heard of the subjunctive at all – think it basically means replacing all their 'if it was's' with 'if it were's', especially in writing. They think it sounds refined, like 'for my brother and I' or 'for he and his sister'. In one of his more recent gritty detective novels, for example, set in Leeds, with a cast of characters not given to verbal delicacy, Peter Robinson has one of his detectives muse, 'If the victim were a prostitute, the chances of finding out where she was were slim.' No, Inspector Banks, you should have mused, 'If the victim was a prostitute, the chances of finding out where she was were slim.' That said, I have to admit that he caught the villain in the end. I've had editors myself in my time who have hunted down 'if it was's' in my manuscripts like ferrets after rabbits – not one was to survive.

Still other English speakers have heard a rumour to the effect that the subjunctive is already defunct – or at least on its very last legs, a terminally enfeebled, clapped-out remnant of an era not even our grandparents can remember, raising its head just once a year on Anzac Day to croak 'forget' after 'lest'. Perhaps if we ignore it, they think, it will quietly turn to dust and give us no more trouble.

All these viewpoints are, I would suggest, misguided. The subjunctive in English, after all, is but a distant cousin of the French – in fact, quite a straightforward, plain-speaking, plucky distant cousin – and there's no evidence at all that it's dying out. Liable to totter and fall over in the wrong company, perhaps, but in full possession of its faculties. In fact, according to the authors of the splendid *Cambridge Grammar of the English Language*, it's actually undergoing something of a revival at the moment. Our grandchildren may well be peppering their speech with it far more often, and more judiciously, than we do.

So what is it? What is the subjunctive – and why are we so leery of it? Well, consider the following sentence: 'The president insisted that all three rogue states have biological weapons.' Now, a native English speaker immediately catches the ambiguity in this sentence: it can mean either that the president is arguing forcibly that these states are now in possession of biological weapons (declaring something to be true, in other words) or that he is anxious for them to acquire them (insisting on their compliance). Somewhere deep in our consciousness (as English speakers in general, I mean, not in the case of airline crews, obviously) lies the conviction that there is an important distinction to be made, through our verbs, between declaring something to be a fact on the one hand ('She sings well' or 'I'm aware of the safety features') and proposing something for consideration on the other, particularly in the sense of expressing a wish for compliance on somebody's part. And not just a wish, but also a request, an order, a vote, a command, or even just discreet advice that somebody *do* (not *does*) something – sing well, be aware of the safety features, acquire biological weapons.

Awkwardly in English, as in the case of the president's insistence that the three rogue states have biological weapons, we don't have a very efficient system of marking our verbs to make it quite clear which mode we're operating in: whether we're declaring something to be so ('North Korea has anthrax') or merely wishing it were so (requiring, recommending, proposing, suggesting or demanding that North Korea *get*, not *gets*, itself some anthrax without delay).

In this situation there are several things we can do: one option is to pretend there isn't really a problem ('I demand that noise levels are kept down', '. . . be kept down' – what does it matter which I say so long as the guy next door stops playing loud music after midnight). Indicative, subjunctive – which I use will hardly be the deciding factor in keeping the noise down, after all, the word 'demand' being pretty unambiguous in itself.

It's after more ambiguous words such as 'insist' or 'suggest' (or 'It's important' or 'vital' or 'appropriate') that misunderstandings are likely to arise. The difference between 'His wife suggested that he always turns the music down after midnight' and 'His wife suggested that he always turn the music down after midnight' could be important in court.

Another thing we can do is make ourselves aware of the tools we do have at our disposal in English to distinguish between declarations of fact and declarations of a wish for compliance (the indicative and subjunctive). Getting it clear in our minds how the subjunctive is formed makes for a good start. Compared to French or Portuguese, it's quite straightforward. Basically, it's what we might call the plain form of the verb without any s's or ed's or ing's added: have, sing, stop, turn, do and so on. The only problem is that it looks or sounds for the most part exactly the same as the present tense of the verb. It's only in the third person singular – after 'he', 'she' and 'it' – where there's now no 's', that we can hear the difference. So, if the president had been speaking about one rogue state, instead of three, his meaning would have been clear: he would have had to insist that North Korea, say, either *has* biological weapons or that it *have* them.

We also know which is which in the case of the verb 'to be'. It's the pedant's delight, the verb 'to be': here 'am', 'is' and 'are' are all replaced by plain old 'be' in the subjunctive, affording us infinite opportunities for finely calibrated distinctions and allowing me, for example, to cavil ungraciously over whether or not the cabin crew thought it was important that I was or that I be aware of how to tie one of those yellow contraptions onto myself and blow my whistle.

If we feel that using the subjunctive for things we'd like to happen sounds too formal, except in minutes of meetings or situations where we're out to impress, we can often resort to other words to help us out: 'can', 'must', 'should', 'ought', 'might', 'may', even 'shall' – auxiliary verbs, as we call them. Our choice depends on how strict our attitude is to compliance with our proposition. 'I suggest we invite the neighbours in for coffee' (subjunctive) sounds more determined than 'I suggest we might invite the neighbours in for coffee.' 'Council recommended that all dogs be kept on a leash' (subjunctive) allows for much less argument than 'Council recommended that all dogs should be kept on a leash.' If Council recommends that all dogs shall be kept on a leash, you gather that, like Jehovah in the Old Testament, it's probably at the end of its tether about a whole lot of things, dogs being just one of them. Only a council ragged with fatigue, however, keen to get home after a long meeting, would issue an edict that all dogs are kept on a leash. Do distinctions of this kind matter? They're always stylish, but sometimes they're indeed crucial to understanding what's being said.

(Now, at this point in my talk I thought that at least half my listeners would have started wondering if it was – yes 'was', not 'were' – time to brush their teeth and put the cat out. We all enjoy mocking cabin crews and watching those who should know better slip on grammatical banana skins, but we don't listen to the radio for lessons in anything. Audiences don't mind learning things, but they can't stand being taught. As my producer once said to me, 'It's not University of the Air, you know.' I was free to edify, but must never teach. And of course he was right. Nowadays the ABC solves this problem either by talking to us as if we were children – even *Gardening Australia* has turned into *Playschool* – or by turning every program it can, however ideas-driven, into a screamingly funny comedy half-hour. In sticky situations I've resorted to these solutions myself. And when you find yourself explaining auxiliary verbs to an audience tempted to put the cat out, you're in a very sticky situation indeed. What they really want to know, I said to myself, before they switch me off, is whether to say 'if I was' or 'if I were'. I brightened my timbre.)

On the 'if I was' or 'if I were' question, here's a rule of thumb: if you're referring to the past, then it's 'was', naturally enough, while if you're actually referring to the present or the future, then it's 'were' (subjunctive). So: 'If Henry was king, it can't have happened in 1548.' But: 'If Henry were still king, he'd have you burnt at the stake.'

We often use the past tense in English to describe an imagined present or future. Have you never wondered why we say, for instance, 'It's time you *went* to bed' even though, quite patently, you haven't yet gone to bed or we wouldn't have had to bring the matter up in the first place. We say, 'Suppose you *flew* to Brisbane next week – you'd be able to see Jack and it would also get you out of the house while my mother's here.' And, meaning 'in future, if you don't mind', we might say, 'I'd rather you *didn't ring* after nine.' In all these dreams of a better future, we use the past tense of the verb. Or so it would appear.

In reality, all these past tenses are subjunctives, if you'll allow me to blow their cover – not that you'd know, except in the case of the pedant's delight: the verb 'to be', when 'was' becomes 'were', as in, 'I wish he weren't married.' We use the subjunctive here because, to our chagrin, he patently is.

We use the past tense (actually subjunctives) in these constructions not in order to ask for compliance, but for a gentler purpose: for the purpose of distance, the distance of politeness, wistfulness, or uncertainty, to suggest another way of picturing the present or the future. So if you're using 'if' just to work out what followed what, if you're merely juggling ideas about what happened in the past, there's no need for a subjunctive. Just say 'was'. Say, for instance: 'If he was never married, then she can't have been his wife.' If, on the other hand, you're using 'if' to posit some completely imagined, even counterfactual scenario for now or later, then replace 'was' with 'were': 'If he were not married – although, tragically, he is – I would be after him like a shot.'

That's why 'if I were you' is always correct if you're talking about the present or future: obviously I'm not you and never will be. And if you're imagining a *past* which never in fact existed, for the sake of distance you just go back one more tense: 'If I'd been you, I'd have bought the green ones.'

~

If only I'd known (not 'knew') what a hodge-podge of ifs and buts my explanation would end up as, I would probably never have embarked upon it. So, at about this point, with a flourish of announcements of what would be on next week, I made a graceful exit, leaving most of my listeners, I'm sure, no wiser than they'd been before I'd begun, although, judging by the volume of mail that came in the following week, in a surprising number of cases obscurely edified. The only other time I can remember receiving such a flurry of responses to a broadcast was when I once castigated a Jewish writer for being rude about Mormons, managing somehow in the process to sound flippant about both camps. Incidentally, the most infuriated letter I ever received as a broadcaster sprang from some other offence I'd committed against religion: a devout Sydney correspondent called upon the Virgin Mary to curse me for whatever it was I'd said. I'm not sure that scattering curses is something Mary is inclined, or in any position, to do, but it was unsettling nonetheless.

The devout were probably put on guard a short time later when I announced that I was going to talk about swearing. Having grown up in a family – indeed, an entire milieu – where nobody swore (at least openly – my father said 'Sugar!' when he lost his self-control – and he'd been a sailor), I've always found foul language vaguely repellent, but intriguing. Who says 'fuck' and 'cunt' (never mind 'shit') and why and when? When I was a child it was only people you came across if you got on the wrong bus – in fact, I was well into high school before I discovered what any of these words actually denoted (what they connoted being perfectly clear) – but these days, as we know, they jump out at us from the television set during prime-time viewing and echo around school playgrounds and the living rooms of even our most genteel friends. Without wanting to make too many teacups rattle, I told my audience, who probably found that old-fashioned expression just as distasteful as 'fuck', I thought it was time for a few frank words on the question of swearing.

Swearing

One of the curious things about *The Bill* on ABC television – you must have noticed – is the way all the police officers, prostitutes and drug addicts in the program, although they don't mind bashing, abusing, robbing and even killing each other, never swear. You might hear a serial murderer shout 'Prat!' or 'Oh, no!' as the police break into his hide-out, but swear? Not even once. You get the impression you could tear these lawbreakers' and law-enforcers' fingernails out one by one and still not a single four-letter word would pass their lips. Almost anything else you can think of does, but no swearwords. It's disarming.

Abusive language is apparently one thing, swearing quite another. We all know why – or think we do: it's the ABC (not SBS), it's family viewing and . . . well, it just wouldn't be right, not in front of the children. This is a curious argument, since even convent girls these days (in my experience on Melbourne trams) seem to have the basics of swearing down pat. But that, as we'll see, is not the point.

To really understand what's going on here, you have to be very clear about the difference between swearing and uttering obscenities, and why almost everybody swears under *certain* circumstances – in English, at least – and, from what I understand, in Spanish under *all* circumstances.

Swearing, as opposed to just saying 'bum' or 'poo' or 'fancy a bonk?', is the use of taboo words (and there are very few of them) either to shock other people (or even yourself) or else as a badge of membership in a peer group, especially in the underworld, bohemia and aggressively working-class environments – any social group that likes to think of itself as thumbing its nose at the respectable majority. Royalty, of course, also swear like troopers. Elizabeth I (I'm not so sure about II) liked nothing better than 'a good mouth-filling oath', as she put it, but this is really just rebelling from above rather than below.

The key words in understanding swearing, as opposed to coarse language or mere profanity, are taboo and shock. Very occasionally we may swear in surprise: you'll remember, I'm sure, the Graham Kennedy anecdote (he told it on air, actually – it was his downfall) about the Australian crow expressing its joy and wonder at the new morning by uttering a common expletive over and over again, although with a particular crow-like croaking sound that made it rhyme with 'lark'. And some people utter swearwords as a matter of course, especially in their own social group or on public transport, while they scrabble around for the next word in the sentence. A nice little labiodental fricative, a gaping vowel and a velar stop give them time to think.

At root, however, to swear is to use a taboo word in order to outrage somebody suddenly – someone you're angry with, someone you resent, even the deity or whoever it was who made you trip over the cat.

The range of swearwords in the modern English-speaking world is tiny. Some claim there's really only one left, one absolutely taboo word (although SBS will sometimes pop it into a subtitle or two) – and that, needless to say, is the one that led to the English dropping the word 'count' (meaning 'nobleman') from their vocabulary, resorting to the Germanic word 'earl' instead. To this day there's something vaguely prissy about 'earl'. Others would suggest a basic list of three words, more or less covering the area of sex and body wastes, while in America it's been customary to speak of the Big Six. They cover the same two areas, plus incest (well, that's still sex, I suppose) and passing wind. In Australia, of course, passing wind is about as offensive as burping.

The point is, obviously, that these words all refer to activities which are taboo in public. It's true that on one episode of *Kath and Kim* there was a spot of horizontal Irish dancing performed in front of an audience of millions, which, I take it, offended very few, but that's presumably because the aim was to amuse, not outrage or bait anybody. These bodily functions aren't taboo in themselves, note: Norman Swan can discuss them on the *Health Report* with impunity, they're discussed on *Life Matters* almost every morning on this very radio station. They're taboo when carried out in public – this is a culture that values very highly indeed the distinction between the public and the private – and certain (not all) words used to describe these functions are also taboo. To use them is a violation of the public self.

Which words evoke this sense of violation depends on the time and place, naturally, as well as the company you're keeping. Why shouting 'intercourse' or 'excrement' is not swearing, whereas shouting one of a handful of short, sharp expletives is swearing, is one of those complicated sociolinguistic phenomena people write doctoral theses on. Why these three or four words out of the scores on offer?

It's not because they're 'ugly' or 'dirty' in themselves – it's merely a convention. There is an interesting theory that it has partly to do with rhythm.

In English we like what's called a good trochee – the pom-de-pom-de metre you hear in 'abso-bloody-lutely' or the American allusion to incest, although Bob Hawke, in his infamous 'silly old bugger' remark, actually opened with a dactyl (pom-de-de), with a trochee to follow. As it happens, the most common English swearwords can readily be adapted to the trochee we're so fond of, which might partly explain the privileged status of this word over that.

Nevertheless, taboos do shift. In fact, most of the words we now use to shock were once thought not particularly shocking or offensive – vulgar, perhaps, in the sense of hardly high-flown, but not shocking. What caused offence four hundred or more years ago was direct reference to God and the Virgin in profane contexts – hence all those 'minced oaths', as they're called, in Shakespeare, all those 'marrys' and 'zounds', some of which have survived – 'bloody', 'gorblimey', 'strewth', 'crikey', 'drat' and 'darn' being a few of the more obvious. What is considered sacred and what profane changes with the times, along with the sense of outrage. As Chesterton once remarked, no one these days can take Odin's name in vain, and, if swearing is any guide, perhaps the Christian panoply of sacred beings is going the same way as Thor and Odin. During the First World War a defendant in the Middlesex Police Court complained quite reasonably that he'd been provoked by being called 'a German and other filthy names'.

I must admit to still feeling affronted by the use of one or two religious terms as expletives, particularly by people who aren't Christians in the first place. I suppose I sense an added layer of contempt for the culture in which I was brought up. I'd be less offended, in other words, if a vicar cried 'Jesus!' as he hit his thumb with a hammer than if a rabbi or imam did.

You get a whiff of the same kind of affront amongst native speakers when a foreigner tries to swear in their mother tongue. A friend of mine, for instance, when young, rather prided himself on the kind of bar-room swearwords he'd mastered while in Russia. (Russian swearwords, by the way, are for the most part all sexual. The Russians sometimes have difficulty subtitling American movies in which the coarse language often refers to excreta and a bodily part no more taboo to a Russian than an elbow would be.)

Anyway, having mastered this inventive array of nouns, verbs and adjectives, he started to sprinkle his speech with them – not to shock, but to show that he was one of the gang. But he wasn't – he was an outsider. Defying Russian linguistic decorum was none of his business. Eventually someone suggested he leave swearing to the natives.

If he'd been baiting them, of course (instead of trying to be one of them), there would have been some point. The natives have always baited foreigners with shocking language (and vice versa), trying to work up a head of steam before a fight. In fact, the Vikings apparently had ritualised swearing tournaments, with one group of combatants hurling streams of hair-raising abuse at its despised opponents, while the Inuit, I gather, are still into it, as well as some Australian Aboriginal clans. Debased forms of this ritual can be seen at football matches (not so much at the cricket), in school playgrounds and shopping malls – wherever clans gather to strut their stuff.

Children goad their parents constantly with challenging language as they get older. Of course it's inappropriate, that's the whole point. It's a vestige of a time when words were less clearly distinguished from actions and even things. To this day in some cultures taboo words are seen as lethal missiles: people will physically duck when sworn at. There's a vestige of that view of words in the two meanings of the English word 'curse'.

Are things any worse today than in yesteryear? Well, yes and no, I'd say. On the face of it, ever since Kenneth Tynan said the 'f' word on the BBC in 1965, it's been all downhill. Some would say it's been all downhill ever since Eliza Doolittle said 'not bloody likely' in 1914 and the Bishop of Woolwich called for a legal ban on the word, but that's probably stretching it. The English poet Philip Larkin probably got the timing more or less right in these well-known lines from a poem called 'Annus mirabilis':

> Sexual intercourse began
> In nineteen sixty-three
> (which was rather late for me) –
> Between the end of the *Chatterley* ban
> and the Beatles' first LP.

And with the explosion of sexual material in the public arena (in songs, plays, novels, on television and so on) came a natural loosening of the decorous restrictions on what you could say in public about this sexual material. Gradually, people began to take pleasure in knocking these restrictions for six by using in public the taboo words for what had itself once been taboo.

As a result, though, almost every single one of these words has lost its status. There's almost nothing I couldn't get away with saying here today on this particular network, where the audience is less mixed than it is for *The Bill* (and so the public space less public). All the same, like Kath and Kim and their horizontal Irish dancing, I'd still have to make sure that you understood I wasn't either baiting you or trying to shock – that I was not swearing, in other words.

Quite some years ago now I was producing a reading from a novel by the Irish writer Roddy Doyle on this station, and the passage I'd chosen, being set in working-class Dublin, was peppered with the 'f' word. Well, we tried it first with a neutral accent – Australian with a sort of lilt – and decided the 'f' word would have to go. But if it went it wouldn't be Roddy Doyle. So the actor pronounced it 'fookin' instead and everyone was happy. Not a single letter of complaint arrived in the office. It was clear now that the word was just a native custom, like a penis-gourd in PNG, and not meant as a slap in the face of public taste.

So has everything gone to the dogs or not? Well, yes, it has, if you believe that the old taboos and the taboo words for them were worth preserving and that in public a strict line should be drawn between private and public usage. (And let's not get too butter-wouldn't-melt-in-my-mouth about private usage. Jane Austen may never have said 'bugger' when she stubbed her toe, but everyone else, from Adam to Doris Day, almost certainly has.) However, if you tend to think that these taboos make no more sense than Elizabethan notions of profanity, you might feel more sanguine about recent developments. There may be more of these words being bandied about, but they've lost almost all their punch, like sex itself.

Less cheerfully, the prevalence of swearing in public spaces might be a sign that we have other things to shock us nowadays and far more deeply than mere words can. Perhaps the face of public taste has grown numb with slapping.

You can be sure of one thing, though: new taboos (and the words to go with them) are just around the corner. Race is looking full of possibilities at the moment. I think you'd find that many younger African-Americans (if that's the term *du jour*) would be far less affronted if I reflected on their close relations with their mother (even the French have adopted that little pearl of abuse) than they would be if I spat out 'sambo' or 'nigger'. Not so long ago Bing Crosby could croon 'nigger', you might remember. Only a black rap singer could get away with it nowadays. That's strutting in front of the clan, however, not swearing.

∽

You just try calling Nelson Mandela 'sambo', though, I'd have liked to add, next time you're out to dinner with your friends, and you'll rattle more than the teacups. But I couldn't say it, not on national radio. The very notion of people like us saying something like that was too shocking. I'd have sooner got away with saying 'fuck'. So, instead, I wondered disingenuously why we'd never been taught to swear in Latin or French at school, never been introduced to the vernacular at all, as a matter of fact, as if the Romans or French spent their lives slaughtering Celts and asking how to get to the Gare du Nord.

One of the reasons was surely that in those days learning a foreign language at school was seen as an 'accomplishment', rather as needlework, say, or learning to play something simple yet melodious on the piano once was for young ladies who actually had no need to be accomplished at either. The vernacular didn't come into it. At university half a century ago it was different: there we were encouraged to believe that foreign languages could be useful, making us more *productive* (although they rarely were or did, because all the useful foreigners started learning English) while at the same time enriching us – not necessarily making us wealthy, but at least enriching us. Learning foreign languages, it was believed, could refine our sensibilities, magnify our humanity, take us on a spiritual adventure that would keep us nourished for the rest of our lives – keep our whole society nourished, as a matter of fact. It sounds quaint now. Not just embarrassingly high-minded, but elitist, self-indulgent, unrealistic, off with the pixies, *quaint*. Universities no longer exist to offer spiritual adventures. Nowadays, if you want to magnify your humanity and go adventuring spiritually, you're expected to do it in your own time – and to avoid the word 'spiritually'. What on earth could reading Lorca in the original do for the corporate balance sheet?

Over two and a half thousand years ago the Greeks (or at least the Athenians) were at each other's throats over precisely this – what is education the key to? One school argued for the legitimacy of learning for learning's sake, for education as the disinterested search for truths (not just facts), for what made the world work and humans human; the other school (the 'pedagogical') favoured learning for material advancement, to acquire wealth and power. Both schools had a point, as they do today. Aristotle helpfully reminded them that you couldn't have civilisation without trade.

The problem for language and literature teachers in our universities today is that they're expected to straddle both concepts of education at a time when the 'pedagogical' arguments for language-learning carry little weight. No one is arguing against the need to inculcate knowledge at the tertiary level – we want it drilled into our dentists and bridge-builders until they drop. The humanities, however, including language departments, are there for a different purpose and there is a sort of barbarism (or at least philistinism, which is barbarism gone middle class) about the notion that their value is of the same order as dentistry's or molecular biology's, that their functions in society are fit to be compared. The life of the mind that the humanities nourish may be impossible without engineers and good dentists, but the life that engineers and dentists make possible is scarcely worth living without a richly informed mental dimension to it. What we think makes for a good education will depend on what we think makes for a good life.

'Richly informed mental dimension': it's embarrassing to have to resort to this sort of pious abstraction. But anything more florid is likely to be openly sneered at. I would like, for instance, to talk about the way that learning French and Russian when I was young was the key to multiple ways of understanding the world; how, once you've read Tolstoy or Flaubert, you will simply love differently, talk differently, reason differently, tell different kinds of jokes, travel through life differently, hunger for things you'd never have known otherwise were there. That sort of talk is liable to be taken about as seriously as Barry Jones's advice to John Howard many years ago: read *War and Peace*, he said, and it might open the door to being a better prime minister. So I'll resist the temptation to indulge in it. Is civilisation dependent on a rich, imaginative life and a rich, imaginative life in its turn on the vivifying effect of loving language? Oh, probably, if we're to take Wittgenstein and his proposal that 'the limits of my language are the limits of my world' seriously. (And I admit I have a quibble with Wittgenstein: all sorts of animals, from parrots to dogs, can clearly picture the world as it is not – and that's a kind of imagination, surely – without language. I don't know about parrots, but Wittgenstein had some decidedly curious ideas about dogs. I don't get the feeling that he was partial to them.) And conversing ceaselessly across generations and borders about the most important things in the world, not just facts, is probably also part of what makes us civilised, and at the very least brilliantly alive, and for that a healthy set of teeth in our mouths and technological sophistication are not sufficient – we need an explosion of languages in our heads. I'd like to talk about these things, but, once my blood was up, I might get up on my high horse and civilisation wouldn't thank me for it.

Besides, I'm well aware that a richly informed mental dimension is nowadays fostered in distressingly few humanities departments, and may just as well spring from an education in science or commerce. I am also aware that if you're an English speaker in the twenty-first century, crossing 'generations and borders' is all too easy without even a smattering of a foreign language. Australians, for example, now live in a distant khanate of the great American English-speaking empire. Empires may be multicultural, but, precisely because they are such a variegated quilt of languages and customs, they generally privilege one or two languages over all the others. In the Roman Empire you'd have had to be highly eccentric to bother learning anything except Latin and Greek (apart from your native tongue). Why would you have learnt Pictish or Aramaic when you could have travelled from the Scottish border to the Euphrates with perfect ease speaking just the two imperial languages? The odd spy or civil servant may have found it judicious to acquire a local dialect or two, but quite frankly, as a Roman vice-chancellor would no doubt have pointed out, there was no great call for Lydian from the Roman business community. And in the early fourteenth century, an Arabic-speaking scholar or trader could move with similar ease within the Dar al-Islam (the House of Islam), speaking Arabic with anyone he needed to make contact with from Spain across to southern China, from the Volga River down to Zanzibar. A spot of Turkish or Persian might have given him an edge here and there, but it was hardly a requirement.

So what should English-speaking travellers do to prepare themselves for jaunts overseas these days? Given that they already speak the world's lingua franca, is there any point in popping a foreign phrasebook into their luggage along with the mosquito repellent and the universal plug? In other words, in the case of an English speaker, what is a phrasebook for? In two minds on the question (as on so many others), in a little radio riff on communicating while travelling abroad, I came up with an alternative to this particular travel accessory. I wonder how many of my listeners took my advice.

On Phrasebooks

So you're off to Thailand for a week or two – or is it Sri Lanka? Being of a friendly disposition, and with an eye to your safety in foreign parts, you thought you'd take along a Thai, or perhaps Sinhala, phrasebook. What a good idea. Except in France, there's nothing the locals are said to warm to more than an attempt to utter a word or two in their language.

On the plane to Bangkok you might like to while away a couple of hours leafing through the thirty or forty pages of introduction. 'It doesn't matter if you failed English grammar,' the author of my Thai phrasebook writes breezily, and grammatically, on page one, 'after all: that's never affected your ability to speak English! You don't need to sit down and memorise endless grammatical details . . . you just need to start speaking.' This is sounding good already – or perhaps even *are* sounding good already, since grammar is just a take-it-or-leave-it frippery.

But you can't, of course, 'just start speaking' Thai without memorising, if not endless, at least certain grammatical details. That's what speaking, as distinct from humming or yelping, *is*, after all: using words grammatically. And you'll need to come to grips, too, with the devilishly complicated Thai tonal system – even my ultra-compact phrasebook devotes several pages to it. Until you master it, you won't, for example, be able to tell the difference between *mài* (low and flat) meaning 'new', *mái* (high and flat) meaning 'wood', *mai* (rising) meaning 'burn' and *mai* meaning several other things (including 'silk' and 'no'), let alone say: 'The new wood won't burn, will it?' (And this, by the way, is as useful a sentence as quite a few of the others in my little book.)

The awkward fact is that Thai and English have utterly dissimilar ways of saying just about everything. The monolingual Australian may be surprised (too late) to learn that you can't just look up the Thai word for 'is', 'that', 'a' and 'scorpion', string them together and come up with a sentence that anyone in Bangkok will react to. Languages don't work like that, as learning English grammar when it was on offer would have made clear.

In Sri Lanka, for instance, if you hanker after any kind of communication more nuanced than a scream, there's no way around it: you'll have to get your teeth into the Sinhala case system. Every noun has nine forms or cases, indicating its relationship to other words in the sentence. Nine. Finnish is far worse, if that makes you feel any better, but, until you know your way around this case system, knowing the word for 'hit', for example, and the word for 'taxi' won't be of much use to you because you won't be able to say whether *you* hit the taxi (which is almost certainly what the driver will allege), or were hit *by* the taxi, or, quite conceivably, *in* the taxi.

In the end you might decide to thumb through quickly to page 178 of your trusty phrasebook (chapter heading: EMERGENCIES) and shout: '*POL-EE-SI-YA-TA ka-thaa ka-ra-na.*' Or, culturally insensitive though it may be, to say, in clear English: 'Please call the police.' Alarmingly, my Sinhala phrasebook then goes on to tell me, in this order, the Sinhala for: 'I know my rights,' 'cell', 'you'll be charged with anti-government activity' and, finally, just before the lights go out, 'paedophilia'.

Which brings me to my main point about phrasebooks: a Mongolian touring Bolivia might see some point in keeping a Mongolian–Quechua phrasebook in his pocket at all times, but on the whole, in countries where the national language is only distantly or not at all related to one's own, and especially where it's written in a different script, the casual English-speaking tourist would be foolish to imagine that a collection of words and phrases for everyday activities, however cleverly it's organised and colour-coded (post office, hotel, health, family, politics, romance and so on), will be of the slightest use whatsoever, except, just possibly, in a dire emergency several hours' drive from the nearest town.

In other words, if you need to refer to a phrasebook in order to convey to the local doctor that you have rabies or venereal disease (items that appear with disconcerting regularity in all my phrasebooks), you may be talking to the wrong doctor. My Thai phrasebook tells me, for instance, how to say, 'I'm crazed with desire, darling', a phrase of limited use anywhere, I'd have thought, but in any case, if I were truly crazed with desire, then, depending on the where and the when of it all . . . Well, you see what I mean, surely. My Sinhala phrasebook, by the way, wisely restricts itself to 'Are you married?'

Traditionally, however, phrasebooks seem to be compiled on the assumption that you'll be using them to engage in all sorts of delicate negotiations you'd in fact need a year of conversation classes to prepare yourself for. 'Would you like to see a good animal film in slow motion?' appears in my German phrasebook, for example, as well as 'Please buy some shipping shares for me,' not to mention 'Do you stock small workboxes with scissors, a thimble, darning material, tape and buttons?' At least it also includes, on a more practical level, 'Beware of the crevasse' and 'I'll take the gooseberries.' Who exactly did the authors imagine would be using their little vade mecum, and in what circumstances?

May I speak frankly? If you want to buy shipping shares in Hamburg or watch animal films in slow motion in Berlin, learn German. And be prepared to speak English with Germans who probably speak it with as much flair as you do. Unless you find yourself a long, long way off the beaten track somewhere far from Western Europe, all the local tour guides, hotel clerks, bus drivers, stallholders, waiters and neatly dressed passers-by will almost certainly speak enough English to help you out, or know somebody who does. And if it's friendship with people of a different culture or meaningful intellectual intercourse you're seeking, I doubt you'll find it flicking through a phrasebook: 'coddled eggs' . . . 'My luggage has been stolen' . . . Hang on! Just a minute! I'm getting there! . . . 'No, this is a *guide* dog' . . . 'I have health insurance' . . . 'Call a lawyer' . . . Ah, yes, here it is: '*GOH-LEE-KA-RA-NA-YA GA-NA O-WUN-GEH*' ('I don't agree with globalisation'). Sorry – I just can't picture it. For this sort of conversation, let's face it, you don't need a phrasebook, you need conversation classes.

For just a couple of weeks' holiday in Sri Lanka – or Argentina, Brazil, Tunisia, wherever you're going – that might seem like too much effort. In that case, anything deep and meaningful you want to say will have to be in English. That's not as insensitive as it sounds: English is not, after all, Samoan or Nepalese, rich and subtle tongues though they may be. It's the world's lingua franca. In fact, it's often quite difficult, if you're keen to converse in the local language, to fend off the crowds (of younger people in particular) eager to practise their English.

Another problem with phrasebooks is this: your everyday activities won't necessarily be mine. My Sri Lankan phrasebook thinks I might need 'I don't mind watching, but I'd prefer not to participate.' And, for argument's sake, I might, but would you?

'I'm Catholic, but not practising,' my Thai phrasebook offers me in Thai – an effervescent little conversation-starter, that one, useless to Presbyterians and distasteful to practising Thai Catholics.

'Where can I buy some lesbian magazines?', 'I smoke pot', 'Where is the Braille library?,' 'Do you play tennis?' – none of these phrases is of the slightest use to me, although one or two of them might be to you . . . But then again, while one should not assume that all tourists are heterosexual and can see, it's difficult to picture the situation in which lesbians or tourists with reading difficulties would resort to a phrasebook to locate their desired reading matter. Rather than accosting strangers in the street, fumbling with your phrasebook, why not call the Tourist Assistance Centre in Bangkok or the Gay Helpline or just google it?

It's true that German, French or Spanish phrasebooks will tend to have more point for us as English speakers than those for languages we're likely to find quite alien. Firstly, the structure of these languages is more familiar, with a lot of shared vocabulary; secondly, we can quickly learn to read notices, street signs and even headlines in the newspapers. So once we can ask our way to the post office in German or Spanish, we can probably quite easily ask our way to the beach or bus stop as well. Once we can say, '*Was wird heute im Theater gespielt?*' ('What's on at the theatre today?'), we won't find saying, '*Was wird heute im Staatstheater gespielt?*' hard to work out for ourselves, or even '*in der Staatsoper*' too difficult. And thirdly, this being a huge advantage, we have a much better chance of understanding at least something of what's said to us in reply. In other words, we can start to play a little in these languages in a short time because quite a few of the basic rules of the game will be the same as in English, or immediately comprehensible. Then we can start to use our phrasebook as a sort of memory prompt as the need arises.

It's not a good idea to get too playful, though. The natives may not be amused. Many guidebooks, as well as the introductions to phrasebooks, suggest that the locals will be delighted by our attempts to limp along in their language. This, I think, is a rosy view of what generally happens. After all, how charmed would you be by a Sri Lankan tourist in Australia reading out 'How many sisters do you have?' from his phrasebook? Indeed, my Quechua phrasebook, to be used in remote Andean villages, states bluntly that walking up to a stranger and starting to speak in Quechua may actually give offence. It's much more polite, apparently, to begin with a little Spanish.

My advice to the holiday-maker wanting some sort of insurance against total incomprehension, some way of signalling an openness to the culture he or she is about to encounter, would be something along these lines: if you're not intending to learn something of the language before you go by taking classes, buying an audio course or working your way through a Teach Yourself book, then take a small piece of cardboard, fold it until it's pocket-sized, and on this piece of cardboard copy from your phrasebook, in whatever way makes the pronunciation easy for you, the local words for greetings, for a few numbers, for dealing with emergencies ('police', 'toilet', 'help!') an interrogative or two ('where', 'when', 'how much?') and a couple of expressions that might roughly translate as 'Just rack off, would you?'. My Sinhala phrasebook proposes some very forceful expressions indeed for dealing with obdurate locals – 'you son of a bitch' is one of the milder ones. In more amicable situations 'Sorry, I don't speak X, but do you speak English?' is always a nice ice-breaker.

It might be an idea to jot down a few phrases to describe where you're from and what you do for a living as well. And in some parts of the world everyone will want to know how many children, brothers, sisters, wives, husbands and in-laws you have and your medical reasons for not having more. Note those down just in case. For other more colourful kinds of relationships, the *Lonely Planet* series, always politically correct to a fault, usually has a range of suggestions.

A phrasebook? I think in most cases you can leave home without it. On the whole, I think you'll find that your little square of cardboard will see you through.

⌒

I've been packing all afternoon for a trip to Portugal, at the far western end of my web of Silk Roads. I've been dreaming in my tower for quite long enough. And now I come to think of it, right from the beginning, ever since my first communion with the Japanese monk Myoe at the far eastern edge of the web – beyond the eastern edge, in fact – Fernando Pessoa has been intruding on my meditations as I drifted westwards.

Before I leave, though, I must find a moment to note down a

few Portuguese expressions on my own little square of cardboard. I doubt that there'll be much call for 'I'm crazed with desire, darling', but 'Are you married?' could be worth jotting down – so brazen, so innocent, it could lead anywhere. Which is what you want in life, surely, and in conversation – even in art, too, although you don't often get it. And then I'll come home, nicely 'thickened', I hope, to feel more at home than ever before.

Lisbon – the city of *saudade*, they say, of the love that remains when whoever or whatever was loved has gone; a higgledy-piggledy city smelling of grilled fish; a city for sauntering or even gallivanting in. It's a place where you can mislay yourself deliciously, as I am now ready to do.

I think I'm going to find myself very interesting indeed in Lisbon.